My Cigar Book

A journal for the cigars you smoke...
for new smokers and daily aficionados

Greg Gonzalo

GO Publishing LLC

WHY KEEP A CIGAR JOURNAL?

HELLO THERE, AMIGOS! AS A NEW CIGAR SMOKER, you're about to embark on a journey of discovering all the unique flavors and experiences that come with trying different cigars. Taking notes on the cigars you try may seem like a tedious task, but it can actually be a fun and helpful way to track your progress and improve your cigar knowledge.

Taking notes can help you remember which cigars you've already tried and whether you enjoyed them or not. With so many different cigars out there, it's easy to forget which ones you've already smoked, and taking notes can help you keep track of what you've already experienced.

Additionally, by jotting down notes on the flavors, aromas, and overall experience of each cigar, you can start to develop a better understanding of what you like and dislike in a cigar. This can help you make more informed choices when selecting cigars in the future and can also be useful when talking to other cigar enthusiasts and getting recommendations.

Furthermore, taking notes can be a fun and social activity. You can share your notes with friends or fellow cigar enthusiasts, compare tasting experiences, and discover new cigars to try. It can also help you develop your personal cigar preferences and enhance your overall enjoyment of smoking cigars.

So let's get started!

What things should I record in my cigar journal?

Keeping a journal of the cigars you smoke can be a helpful way to remember which cigars you've enjoyed and which ones you didn't, and it can also be a fun way to track your progress as a cigar smoker. Here are some aspects of the cigar-smoking experience that are worth recording in your journal:

Cigar Details

Be sure to note the cigar's name, brand, size, country of origin, and any other pertinent details about the cigar.

Ring gauge and length are two important measurements describing a cigar's size and shape.

Ring gauge refers to the diameter of a cigar, measured in 64ths of an inch. For example, a cigar with a ring gauge of 48 has a diameter of 48/64 or 3/4 of an inch. The ring gauge can affect how a cigar draws and its smoking time. A cigar with a larger ring gauge generally has a slower burn and a looser draw, while a cigar with a smaller ring gauge will burn faster and have a tighter draw. The ring gauge can also affect the flavor profile of a cigar, with thicker cigars generally being fuller in flavor and thinner cigars milder.

Length refers to the overall size of a cigar, measured in inches. The length of a cigar can affect the smoking time and the flavor profile. Longer cigars will generally take longer to smoke, while shorter cigars will burn more quickly. The length of a cigar can also affect how the flavors develop over the smoke. For example, a longer cigar may start off mild and develop into a stronger flavor, while a shorter cigar may offer a more intense flavor from the start.

Together, a cigar's ring gauge and length can give you a good idea of its overall smoking experience. It's important to consider both measurements when selecting a cigar, as they can affect how it draws, burns, and tastes.

APPEARANCE

Record your initial impressions of the cigar's appearance, including the wrapper, band, and overall construction.

Here are some things to look for when examining the appearance of a cigar:

- Wrapper: The wrapper is the outermost layer of the cigar and can come in various shades, from light tan to dark brown and even green or striped! A smooth, even wrapper with minimal veins can indicate high-quality tobacco and careful construction. Wrappers can affect the flavor of a cigar, with darker wrappers generally offering a more intense flavor.
- Cap: The cap is the part of the cigar that is cut before smoking. A well-made cap should be uniform and secure, with no frayed edges. A poorly made cap can lead to unraveling and an uneven burn.
- Shape: As I mentioned earlier, cigars come in different shapes, which can affect the smoking experience. The large majority of cigars have a "parejo" shape—cylindrical, and rounded on one end. Other cigars are flared at one of both ends, or even braided.
- Construction: A well-constructed cigar will feel firm to the touch, with no soft spots or lumps. The foot of the cigar should be packed tightly, with no air pockets. A poorly constructed cigar can burn unevenly and affect the flavor and draw.

All of these aspects of a cigar's appearance can affect the smoking experience. A well-made cigar with a high-quality wrapper and construction will generally offer a better draw and burn and a more enjoyable flavor. A poorly made cigar may burn unevenly, have a tight or loose draw, or offer a less pleasant flavor. It's important to examine the appearance of a cigar before smoking it to get a sense of its overall quality and potential smoking experience.

PRE-LIGHT

Before lighting the cigar, record any aromas you detect from the wrapper and foot of the cigar. You can also note the cold draw and any flavors you pick up.

The pre-light inspection of a cigar is an important step in the smoking process, as it can give you clues about the cigar's construction, flavor profile, and potential smoking experience. Here are some things to look for during the pre-light inspection:

- Appearance: As I mentioned earlier, the appearance of a cigar can tell you a lot about its construction and potential smoking experience. Look for a well-made cap, a smooth and even wrapper, and a firm construction without any soft spots or lumps.
- Aroma: Before lighting a cigar, take a few sniffs of the foot and wrapper to get a sense of its aroma. The aroma can offer clues about the cigar's flavor profile, with notes of coffee, cocoa, or cedar indicating a fuller flavor, while notes of hay or grass may suggest a milder flavor.

- Cold Draw: The cold draw is the process of puffing on an unlit cigar to get a sense of its draw and flavor. The cold draw can offer clues about the cigar's draw and flavor, with a tight or loose draw indicating potential construction issues, and a rich, complex flavor suggesting a high-quality tobacco blend.
- Moisture: It's important to check the moisture level of a cigar before smoking it. A dry cigar can burn too quickly and offer a harsh, unpleasant flavor, while an overly moist cigar may be difficult to light and can produce a bitter taste.
- Foot: Finally, examine the foot of the cigar to make sure it is properly packed and without any air pockets or damage. A well-packed foot will offer a better draw and more even burn.

By examining these aspects of a cigar during the pre-light inspection, you can get a good sense of its potential smoking experience. A well-made cigar with a pleasant aroma, good draw, and proper moisture level will generally offer a more enjoyable smoking experience, with a complex flavor profile and even burn.

Lighting

Record how the cigar lit, and if you noticed any flavors or changes during the first few puffs.

Taking notes on the lighting and first few puffs of a cigar is an important step in evaluating its flavor and overall smoking experience. Here are some things to look for when taking notes on the lighting and first few puffs of a cigar:

- Lighting: The lighting process can affect the overall smoking experience of a cigar. A well-lit cigar should have an even burn with a smooth and steady draw. Make note of how many times you need to relight the cigar and whether it is easy or difficult to keep the cigar lit.
- First Puffs: The first few puffs of a cigar can offer important clues about its flavor profile. Note the initial flavors that you taste, including any sweetness, spice, or bitterness. Take note of the strength of the cigar, whether it is mild, medium, or full-bodied.
- Smoke Quality: The smoke quality can also affect the overall smoking experience of a cigar. Take note of the smoke volume, density, and texture. A well-made cigar should produce a thick, creamy smoke with a pleasant aroma.
- Draw: The draw of a cigar can also affect the overall smoking experience. Note whether the draw is tight or loose and whether it affects the overall flavor and smoke quality.
- Burn: Finally, note the burn of the cigar, including whether it is even or uneven, and whether it requires any touch-ups. An uneven burn can affect

the flavor profile of a cigar, while frequent touch-ups can indicate construction issues.

By taking notes on these aspects of the lighting and first few puffs of a cigar, you can begin to evaluate its overall quality and potential smoking experience. A well-made cigar with a smooth draw, even burn, and pleasant flavor profile will generally offer a more enjoyable smoking experience.

Flavor Profiles

Note the flavors you detect throughout the cigar-smoking experience, including any changes in flavor or intensity. You can use descriptive terms like sweet, spicy, woody, or nutty to help you remember the flavors.

Describing the flavor profile of a cigar can be challenging, as there are many subtle nuances and complexities that can be difficult to articulate. However, with practice and a bit of guidance, new cigar smokers can learn to discern the flavors of a cigar. Here are some hints and tips to help you identify the flavors of a cigar:

- Take your time: It's important to take your time when smoking a cigar, as flavors can change and develop over the course of the smoke. Take small, slow puffs to allow the smoke to linger on your palate and taste buds.

- Pay attention to the aroma: The aroma of a cigar can offer important clues about its flavor profile. Take a few deep sniffs of the smoke and try to identify any notes of coffee, cocoa, cedar, earth, or other scents.
- Look for common flavors: Some common flavors found in cigars include leather, pepper, wood, earth, and nuts. Try to identify these flavors in the smoke and take note of their intensity and complexity.
- Try retrohaling: Retrohaling is the process of exhaling smoke through your nose, which can help you identify subtle flavors and aromas. Take a small puff of smoke and exhale it slowly through your nose.
- Experiment with pairings: Pairing a cigar with a complimentary beverage, such as coffee, whiskey, or red wine, can help enhance the flavors and aromas of the smoke. Take note of how the pairing affects the overall smoking experience.
- Use a flavor wheel: A flavor wheel is a tool that can help you identify and describe the flavors of a cigar. It provides a visual guide to the different flavor categories, such as sweet, spicy, and earthy, and can help you identify specific flavor notes within each category.

You can easily find these flavor wheels online. Here is a breakdown of the different sections of the flavor wheel:

- Sweet: This category includes flavors such as honey, caramel, vanilla, and cocoa.
- Spicy: This category includes flavors such as black pepper, cinnamon, and nutmeg.
- Earthy: This category includes flavors such as leather, cedar, and earth.
- Woody: This category includes flavors such as oak, hickory, and mesquite.
- Nutty: This category includes flavors such as almond, walnut, and hazelnut.
- Herbal: This category includes flavors such as mint, sage, and thyme.
- Floral: This category includes flavors such as rose, jasmine, and lavender.
- Fruity: This category includes flavors such as citrus, berry, and apple.
- Vegetal: This category includes flavors such as grass, hay, and tea.

Within each category, there are several subcategories that offer more specific flavors. For example, the sweet category includes subcategories such as honey, caramel, vanilla, and cocoa, while the spicy category includes subcategories such as black pepper, cinnamon, and nutmeg. By using the flavor wheel, cigar smokers can identify and describe the specific flavor notes they detect in a cigar, which can help them better appreciate and evaluate the smoking experience.

Remember, identifying the flavors of a cigar is a skill that takes practice and experience. Don't be afraid to experiment with different cigars, take notes on their flavor profiles, and seek out guidance from more experienced smokers. Over time, you will develop a better understanding and appreciation for the complex flavors and aromas of a fine cigar.

STRENGTH

Record how strong the cigar felt to you, whether it was mild, medium, or full-bodied.

In cigars, the term "strength" typically refers to the intensity of the nicotine content in the smoke. This can affect the overall smoking experience, as the strength of the cigar can impact the body and the mind in different ways. Discerning the strength of a cigar can be subjective, as it can vary depending on factors such as the smoker's tolerance, the size of the cigar, and the blend of the tobacco.

Here are some tips for discerning and describing the strength of a cigar:

- Start with a mild cigar: If you are new to cigars, it's best to start with a mild cigar to get a sense of what "strength" means in this context. A mild cigar will have a lower nicotine content and a more subtle flavor profile, which can help you build up your tolerance and palate.

- Take note of the nicotine buzz: Nicotine can have a stimulating effect on the body and mind, and a stronger cigar can produce a more pronounced "buzz." Pay attention to how the cigar affects your body and mind, and take note of any changes in your perception or energy levels.
- Use a strength scale: Many cigar enthusiasts use a strength scale to describe the intensity of a cigar. This can range from mild to full-bodied, or from one to five in terms of strength.
- Look for flavor cues: The flavor profile of a cigar can also provide cues about its strength. For example, a cigar with stronger, spicier flavors may be perceived as stronger overall, while a cigar with milder, sweeter flavors may be perceived as less strong.

Remember, discerning and describing the strength of a cigar is a skill that takes practice and experience. By starting with milder cigars, paying attention to the body and nicotine buzz, using a strength scale, and taking note of the flavor profile, you can begin to develop a better understanding and appreciation for the range of strengths found in cigars.

BURN AND DRAW

Note how the cigar burned, if it required any touch-ups, and if the draw was loose or tight.

- Burn: The burn of a cigar refers to how evenly the tobacco burns and how well the ash holds together. A good burn should be even and slow, and the ash should be firm and hold together well. A poor burn can lead to uneven or tunneling burn, which can affect the flavor and overall experience of the cigar.
- Draw: The draw of a cigar refers to how easily the smoke is drawn through the cigar. A good draw should be smooth and easy without being too loose or too tight. A tight draw can make it difficult to get a good amount of smoke, while a loose draw can lead to a fast burn and hot smoke.

If the burn or draw of a cigar is off, it can affect the flavor and overall enjoyment of the smoking experience. For example, if the burn is uneven or the ash falls apart easily, it can create a bitter taste and an unpleasant smoking experience. Similarly, if the draw is too tight or too loose, it can affect the temperature of the smoke and the amount of smoke you're able to get, which can impact the flavor and aroma of the cigar.

It's important to pay attention to the burn and draw of a cigar while smoking it. If you notice any issues with the burn or draw, try adjusting the way you're smoking the cigar (such as puffing less frequently or more slowly), or consider trying a different cigar with a different blend or size. By paying attention to the burn and draw, you can ensure that you get the most out of your smoking experience and enjoy the full flavor profile of the cigar.

OVERALL EXPERIENCE

Sum up your overall experience with the cigar, noting whether you enjoyed it or not and why.

Remember that everyone's palate is different, so the flavors and experiences you detect may be different from others. The important thing is to record what you experienced and what you enjoyed so that you can build your knowledge and preferences as a cigar smoker. A rating system is always a good idea, so you can quickly look at your next time you're choosing a cigar, and remember your favorites.

CIGAR JOURNAL

TAPE YOUR CIGAR BAND HERE

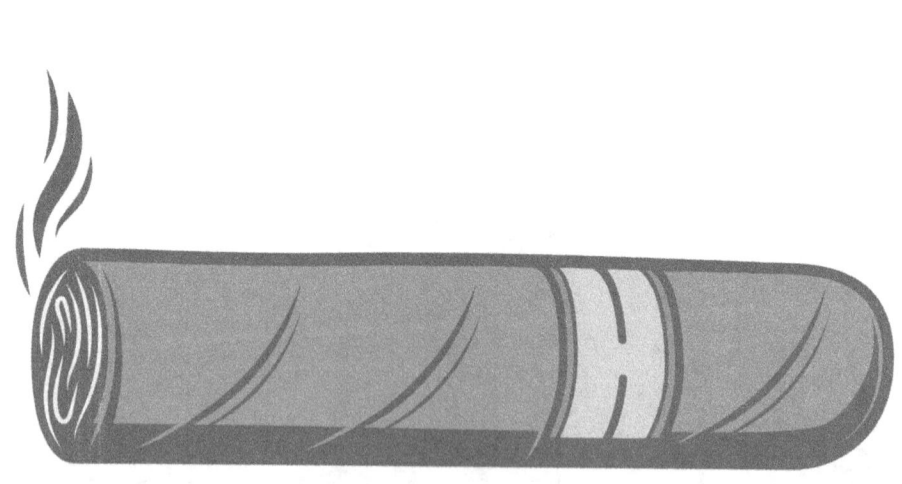

TODAY'S CIGAR:

SIZE/SHAPE:

COUNTRY OF ORIGIN:

APPEARANCE:

PRE-LIGHT:

LIGHTING:

FLAVORS:

FIRST THIRD-

SECOND THIRD-

FINAL THIRD-

STRENGTH: **MILD - MEDIUM - FULL**

BURN / DRAW:

NOTES:

GRADE (0-100):

TAPE YOUR CIGAR BAND HERE

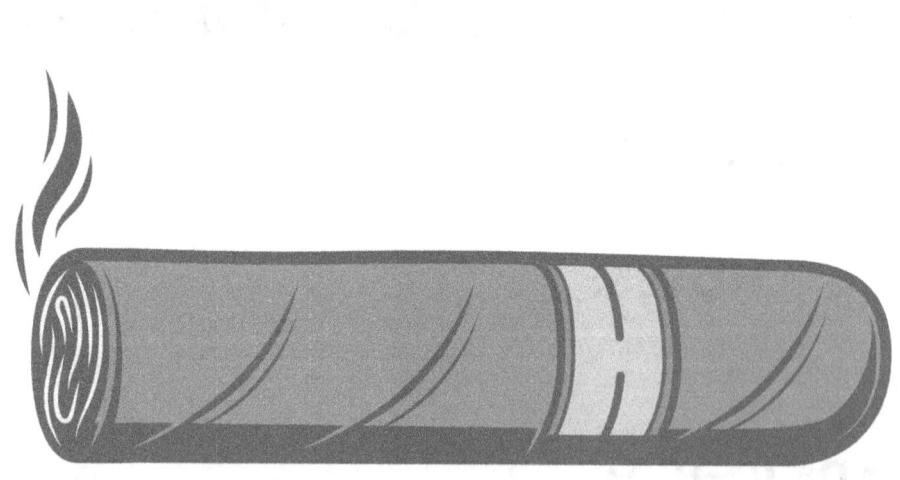

TODAY'S CIGAR:

SIZE/SHAPE:

COUNTRY OF ORIGIN:

APPEARANCE:

PRE-LIGHT:

LIGHTING:

FLAVORS:

FIRST THIRD-

SECOND THIRD-

FINAL THIRD-

STRENGTH: **MILD - MEDIUM - FULL**

BURN / DRAW:

NOTES:

GRADE (0-100):

TAPE YOUR CIGAR BAND HERE

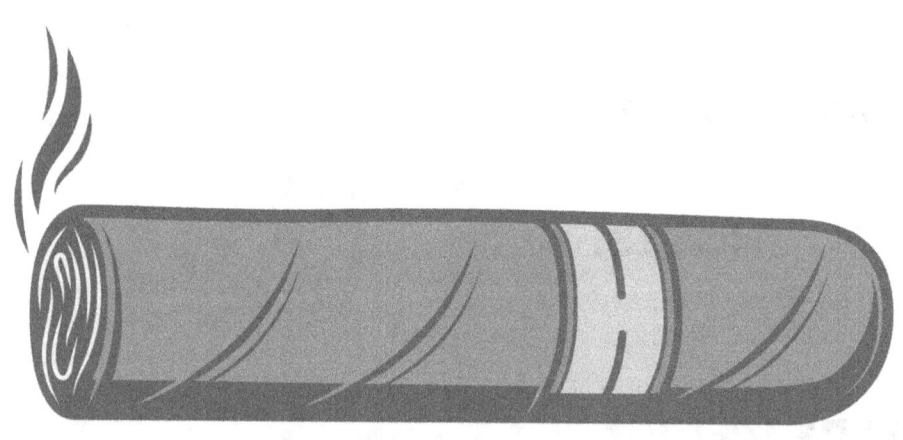

TODAY'S CIGAR:

SIZE/SHAPE:

COUNTRY OF ORIGIN:

APPEARANCE:

PRE-LIGHT:

LIGHTING:

FLAVORS:
FIRST THIRD-
SECOND THIRD-
FINAL THIRD-

STRENGTH: **MILD - MEDIUM - FULL**

BURN / DRAW:

NOTES:

GRADE (0-100):

TAPE YOUR CIGAR BAND HERE

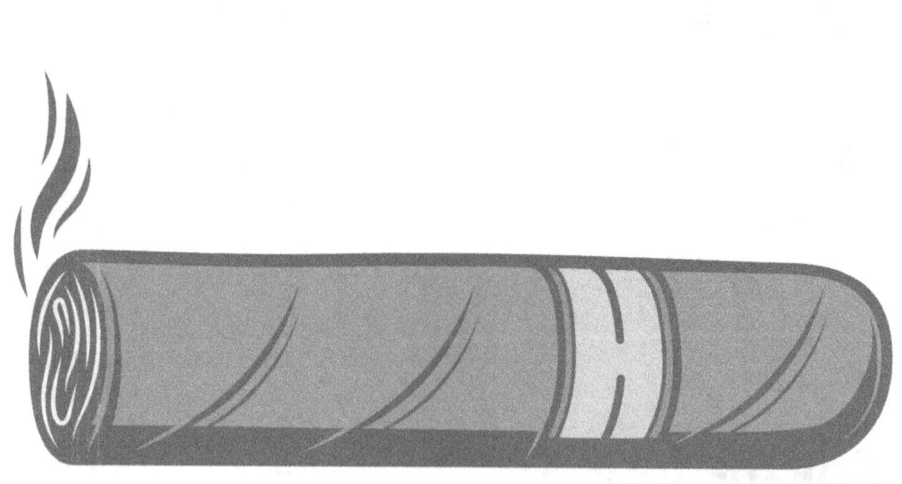

TODAY'S CIGAR:

SIZE/SHAPE:

COUNTRY OF ORIGIN:

APPEARANCE:

PRE-LIGHT:

LIGHTING:

FLAVORS:

FIRST THIRD-

SECOND THIRD-

FINAL THIRD-

STRENGTH: **MILD - MEDIUM - FULL**

BURN / DRAW:

NOTES:

GRADE (0-100):

TAPE YOUR CIGAR BAND HERE

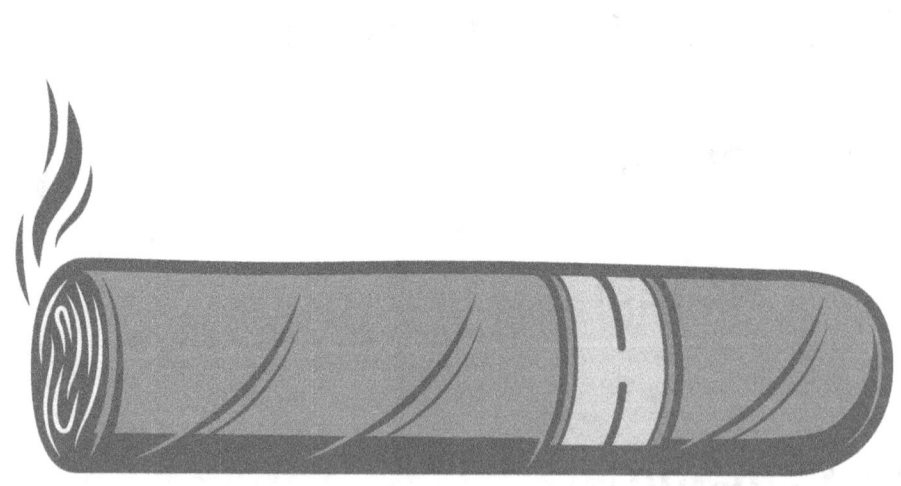

TODAY'S CIGAR:

SIZE/SHAPE:

COUNTRY OF ORIGIN:

APPEARANCE:

PRE-LIGHT:

LIGHTING:

FLAVORS:

FIRST THIRD-

SECOND THIRD-

FINAL THIRD-

STRENGTH: **MILD - MEDIUM - FULL**

BURN / DRAW:

NOTES:

GRADE (0-100):

TAPE YOUR CIGAR BAND HERE

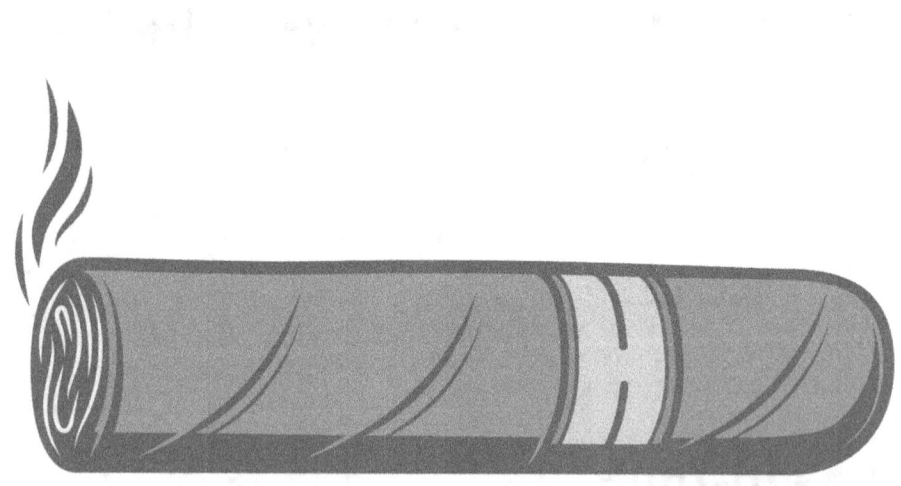

TODAY'S CIGAR:

SIZE/SHAPE:

COUNTRY OF ORIGIN:

APPEARANCE:

PRE-LIGHT:

LIGHTING:

FLAVORS:

FIRST THIRD-

SECOND THIRD-

FINAL THIRD-

STRENGTH: **MILD - MEDIUM - FULL**

BURN / DRAW:

NOTES:

GRADE (0-100):

TAPE YOUR CIGAR BAND HERE

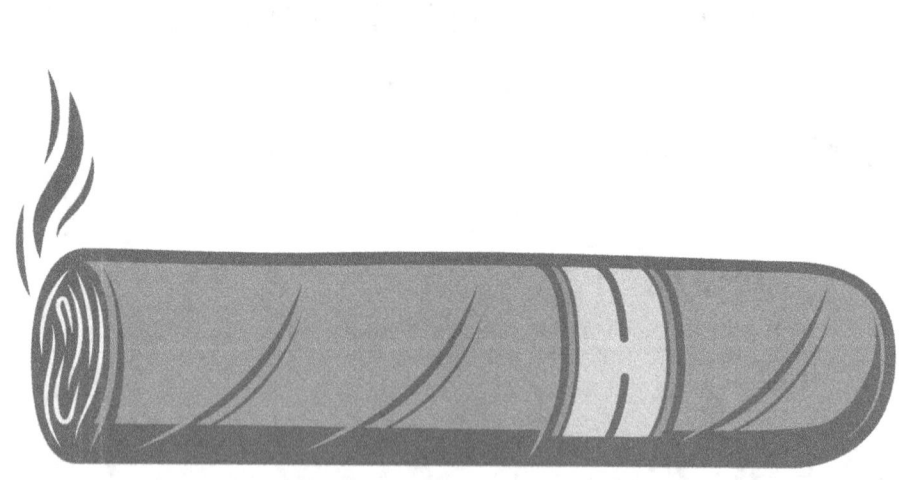

TODAY'S CIGAR:

SIZE/SHAPE:

COUNTRY OF ORIGIN:

APPEARANCE:

PRE-LIGHT:

LIGHTING:

FLAVORS:

FIRST THIRD-

SECOND THIRD-

FINAL THIRD-

STRENGTH: **MILD - MEDIUM - FULL**

BURN / DRAW:

NOTES:

GRADE (0-100):

TAPE YOUR CIGAR BAND HERE

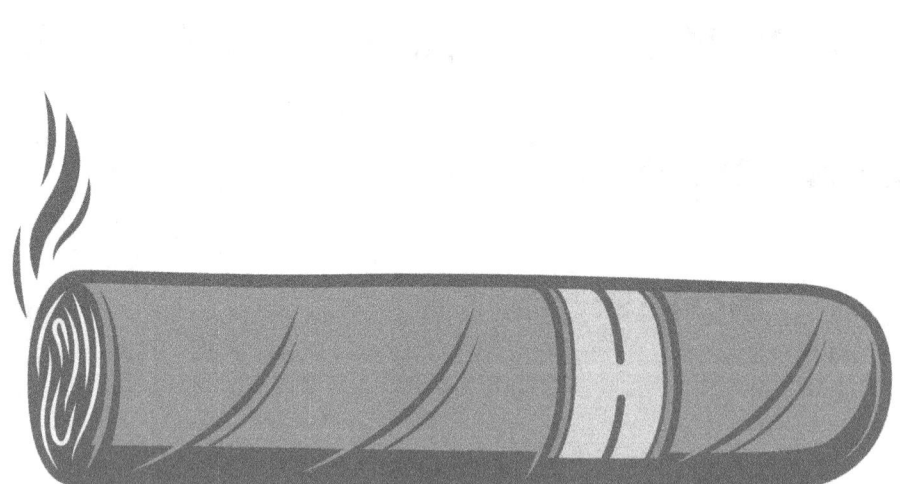

TODAY'S CIGAR:

SIZE/SHAPE:

COUNTRY OF ORIGIN:

APPEARANCE:

PRE-LIGHT:

LIGHTING:

FLAVORS:
FIRST THIRD-
SECOND THIRD-
FINAL THIRD-

STRENGTH: **MILD - MEDIUM - FULL**

BURN / DRAW:

NOTES:

GRADE (0-100):

TAPE YOUR CIGAR BAND HERE

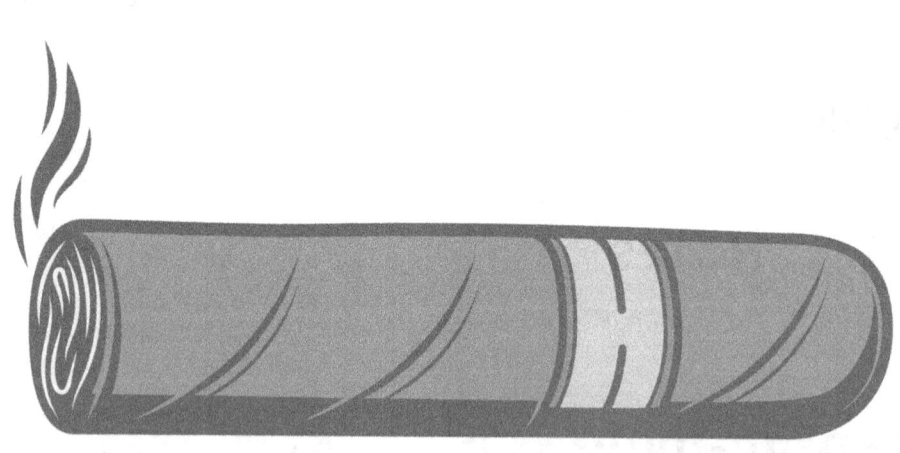

TODAY'S CIGAR:

SIZE/SHAPE:

COUNTRY OF ORIGIN:

APPEARANCE:

PRE-LIGHT:

LIGHTING:

FLAVORS:

FIRST THIRD-

SECOND THIRD-

FINAL THIRD-

STRENGTH: **MILD - MEDIUM - FULL**

BURN / DRAW:

NOTES:

GRADE (0-100):

TAPE YOUR CIGAR BAND HERE

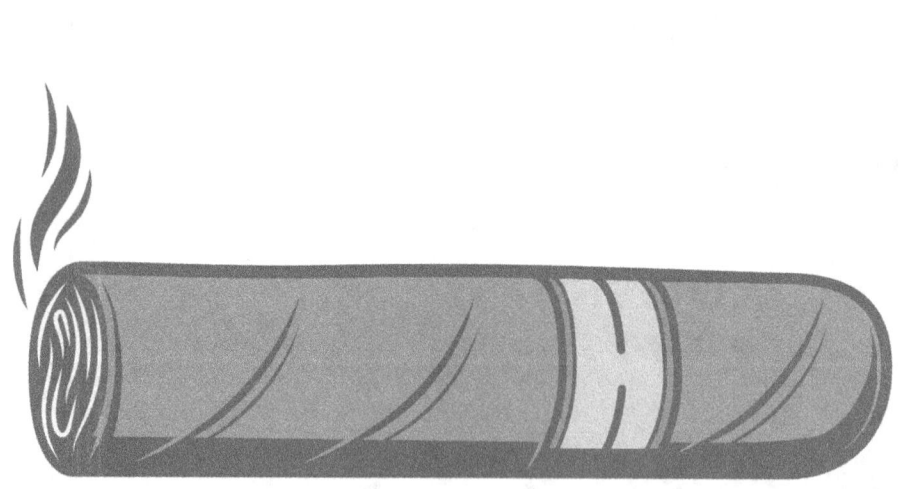

TODAY'S CIGAR:

SIZE/SHAPE:

COUNTRY OF ORIGIN:

APPEARANCE:

PRE-LIGHT:

LIGHTING:

FLAVORS:

FIRST THIRD-

SECOND THIRD-

FINAL THIRD-

STRENGTH: **MILD - MEDIUM - FULL**

BURN / DRAW:

NOTES:

GRADE (0-100):

TAPE YOUR CIGAR BAND HERE

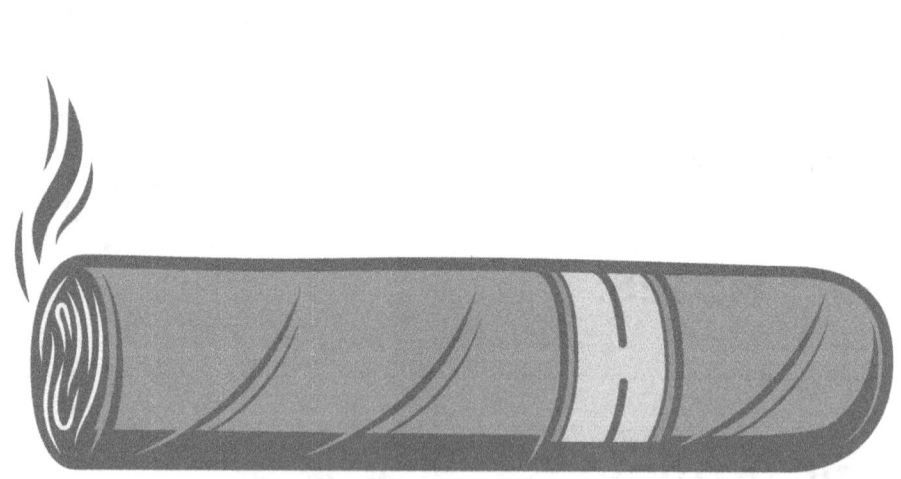

TODAY'S CIGAR:

SIZE/SHAPE:

COUNTRY OF ORIGIN:

APPEARANCE:

PRE-LIGHT:

LIGHTING:

FLAVORS:

FIRST THIRD-

SECOND THIRD-

FINAL THIRD-

STRENGTH: **MILD - MEDIUM - FULL**

BURN / DRAW:

NOTES:

GRADE (0-100):

TAPE YOUR CIGAR BAND HERE

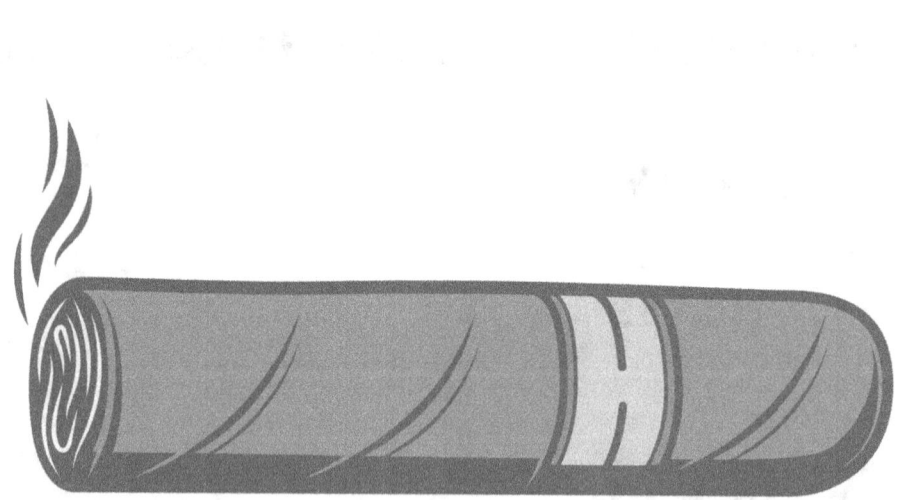

TODAY'S CIGAR:

SIZE/SHAPE:

COUNTRY OF ORIGIN:

APPEARANCE:

PRE-LIGHT:

LIGHTING:

FLAVORS:

FIRST THIRD-

SECOND THIRD-

FINAL THIRD-

STRENGTH: **MILD - MEDIUM - FULL**

BURN / DRAW:

NOTES:

GRADE (0-100):

TAPE YOUR CIGAR BAND HERE

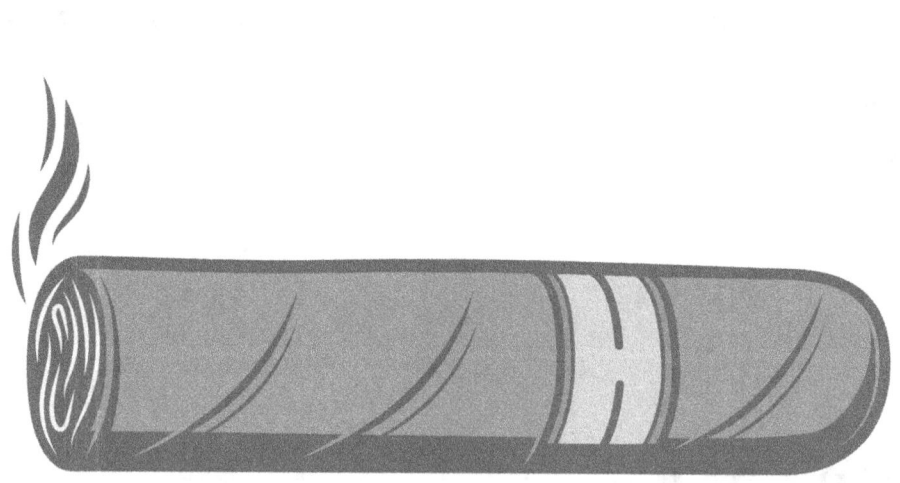

TODAY'S CIGAR:

SIZE/SHAPE:

COUNTRY OF ORIGIN:

APPEARANCE:

PRE-LIGHT:

LIGHTING:

FLAVORS:

FIRST THIRD-

SECOND THIRD-

FINAL THIRD-

STRENGTH: MILD - MEDIUM - FULL

BURN / DRAW:

NOTES:

GRADE (0-100):

TAPE YOUR CIGAR BAND HERE

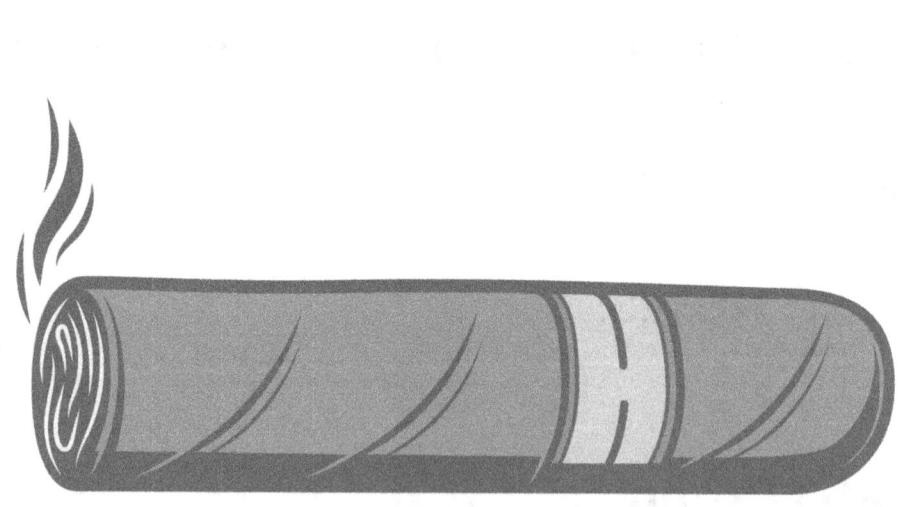

TODAY'S CIGAR:

SIZE/SHAPE:

COUNTRY OF ORIGIN:

APPEARANCE:

PRE-LIGHT:

LIGHTING:

FLAVORS:

FIRST THIRD-

SECOND THIRD-

FINAL THIRD-

STRENGTH: MILD - MEDIUM - FULL

BURN / DRAW:

NOTES:

GRADE (0-100):

TAPE YOUR CIGAR BAND HERE

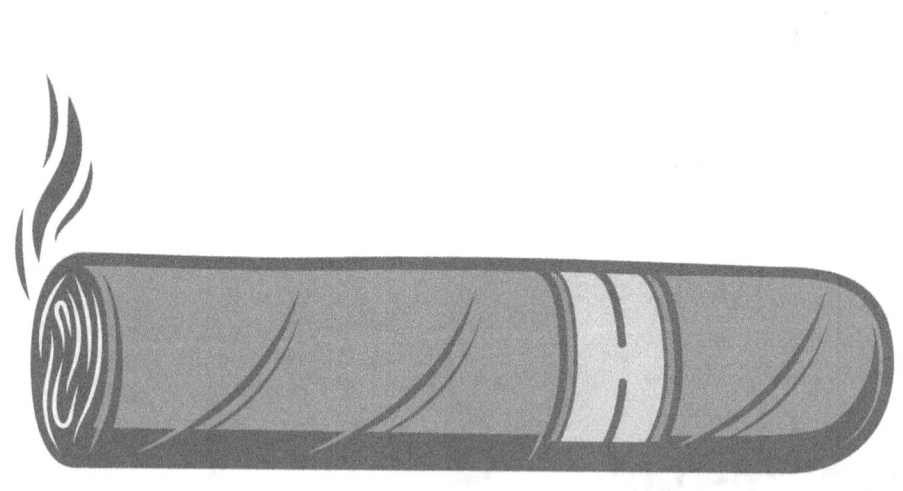

TODAY'S CIGAR:

SIZE/SHAPE:

COUNTRY OF ORIGIN:

APPEARANCE:

PRE-LIGHT:

LIGHTING:

FLAVORS:
FIRST THIRD-
SECOND THIRD-
FINAL THIRD-

STRENGTH: **MILD - MEDIUM - FULL**

BURN / DRAW:

NOTES:

GRADE (0-100):

TAPE YOUR CIGAR BAND HERE

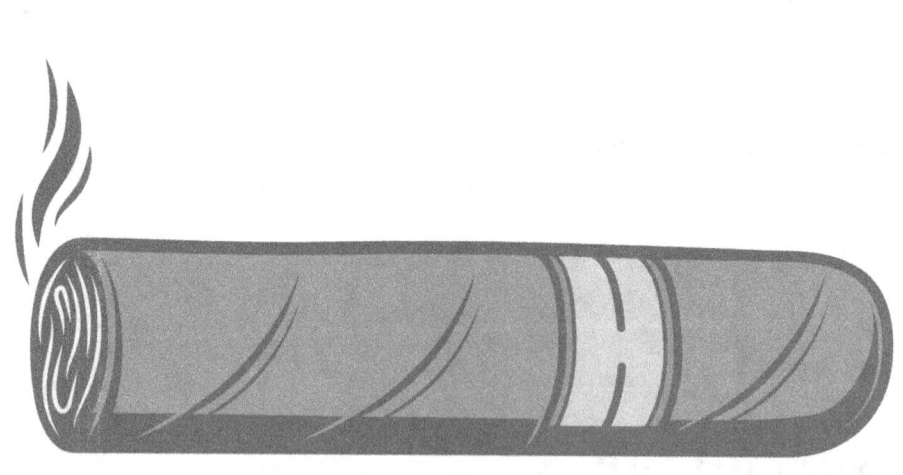

TODAY'S CIGAR:

SIZE/SHAPE:

COUNTRY OF ORIGIN:

APPEARANCE:

PRE-LIGHT:

LIGHTING:

FLAVORS:

FIRST THIRD-

SECOND THIRD-

FINAL THIRD-

STRENGTH: **MILD - MEDIUM - FULL**

BURN / DRAW:

NOTES:

GRADE (0-100):

TAPE YOUR CIGAR BAND HERE

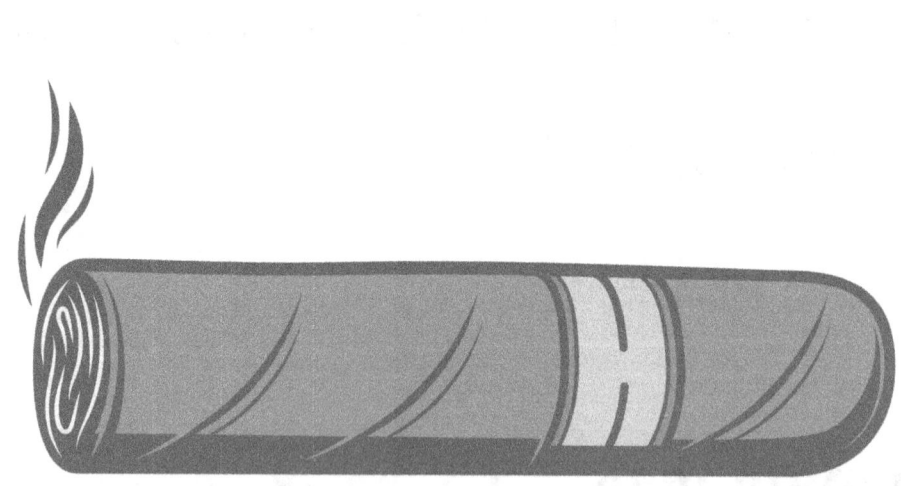

TODAY'S CIGAR:

SIZE/SHAPE:

COUNTRY OF ORIGIN:

APPEARANCE:

PRE-LIGHT:

LIGHTING:

FLAVORS:

FIRST THIRD-

SECOND THIRD-

FINAL THIRD-

STRENGTH: **MILD - MEDIUM - FULL**

BURN / DRAW:

NOTES:

GRADE (0-100):

TAPE YOUR CIGAR BAND HERE

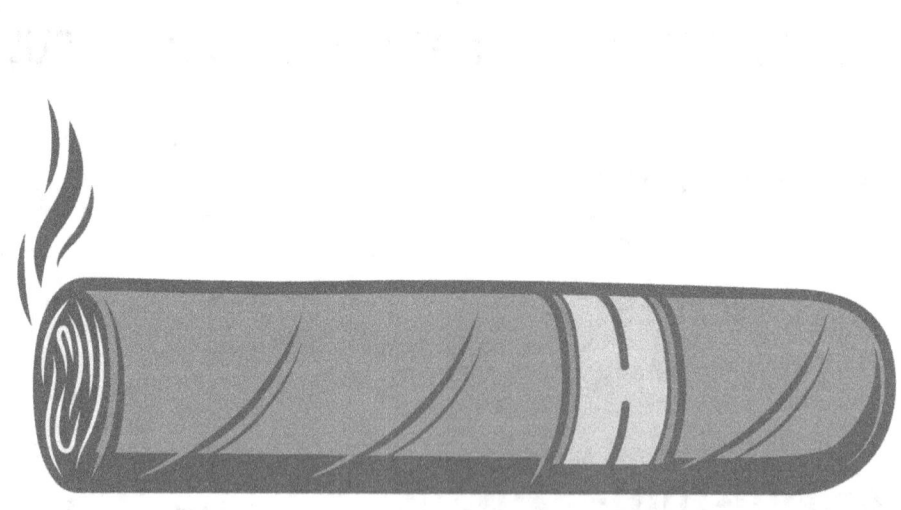

TODAY'S CIGAR:

SIZE/SHAPE:

COUNTRY OF ORIGIN:

APPEARANCE:

PRE-LIGHT:

LIGHTING:

FLAVORS:

FIRST THIRD-

SECOND THIRD-

FINAL THIRD-

STRENGTH: **MILD - MEDIUM - FULL**

BURN / DRAW:

NOTES:

GRADE (0-100):

TAPE YOUR CIGAR BAND HERE

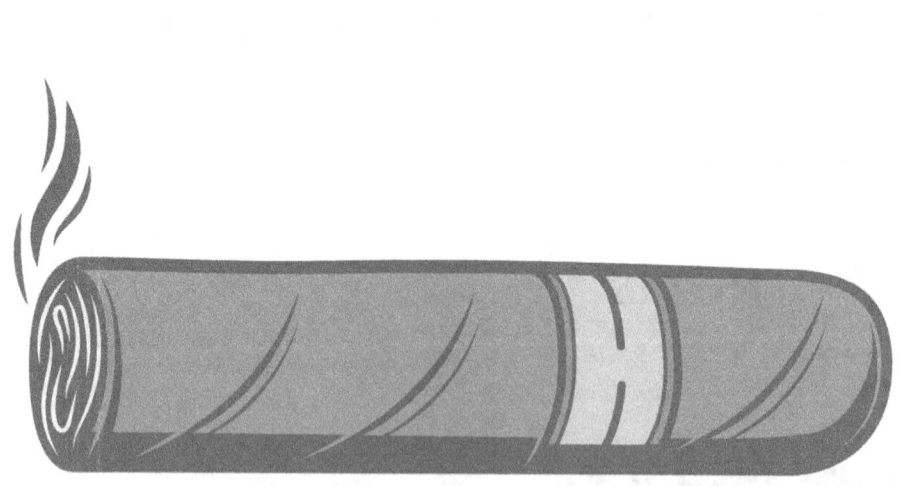

TODAY'S CIGAR:

SIZE/SHAPE:

COUNTRY OF ORIGIN:

APPEARANCE:

PRE-LIGHT:

LIGHTING:

FLAVORS:

FIRST THIRD-

SECOND THIRD-

FINAL THIRD-

STRENGTH: **MILD - MEDIUM - FULL**

BURN / DRAW:

NOTES:

GRADE (0-100):

TAPE YOUR CIGAR BAND HERE

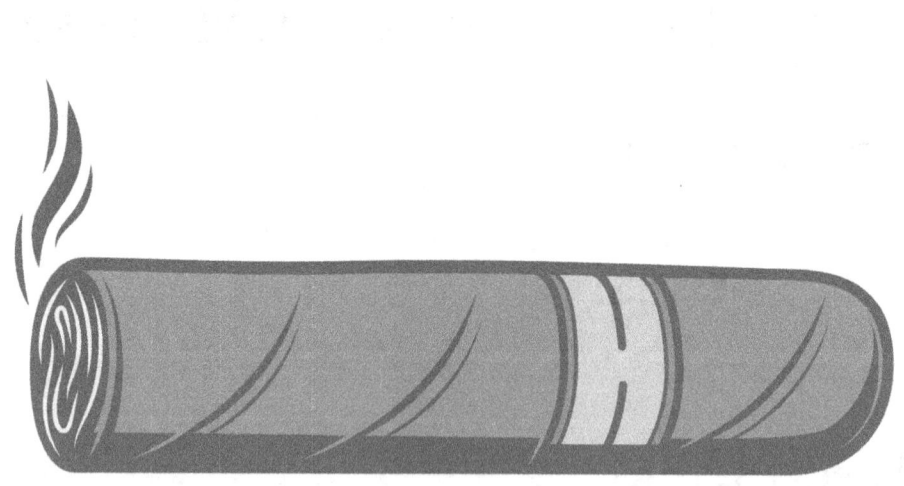

TODAY'S CIGAR:

SIZE/SHAPE:

COUNTRY OF ORIGIN:

APPEARANCE:

PRE-LIGHT:

LIGHTING:

FLAVORS:

FIRST THIRD-

SECOND THIRD-

FINAL THIRD-

STRENGTH: **MILD - MEDIUM - FULL**

BURN / DRAW:

NOTES:

GRADE (0-100):

TAPE YOUR CIGAR BAND HERE

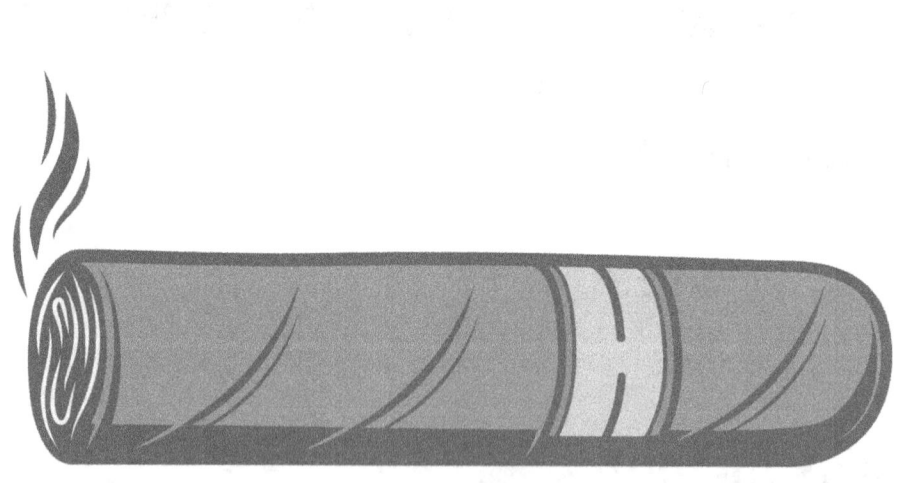

TODAY'S CIGAR:

SIZE/SHAPE:

COUNTRY OF ORIGIN:

APPEARANCE:

PRE-LIGHT:

LIGHTING:

FLAVORS:

FIRST THIRD-

SECOND THIRD-

FINAL THIRD-

STRENGTH: **MILD - MEDIUM - FULL**

BURN / DRAW:

NOTES:

GRADE (0-100):

TAPE YOUR CIGAR BAND HERE

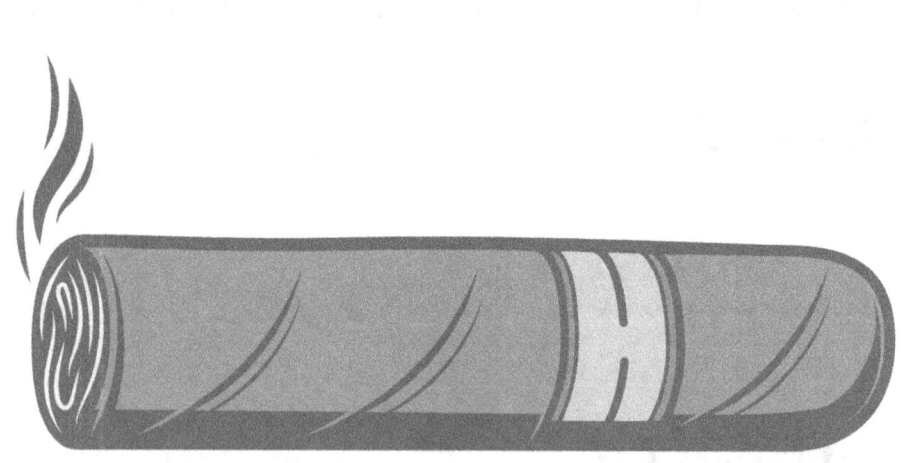

TODAY'S CIGAR:

SIZE/SHAPE:

COUNTRY OF ORIGIN:

APPEARANCE:

PRE-LIGHT:

LIGHTING:

FLAVORS:

FIRST THIRD-

SECOND THIRD-

FINAL THIRD-

STRENGTH: **MILD - MEDIUM - FULL**

BURN / DRAW:

NOTES:

GRADE (0-100):

TAPE YOUR CIGAR BAND HERE

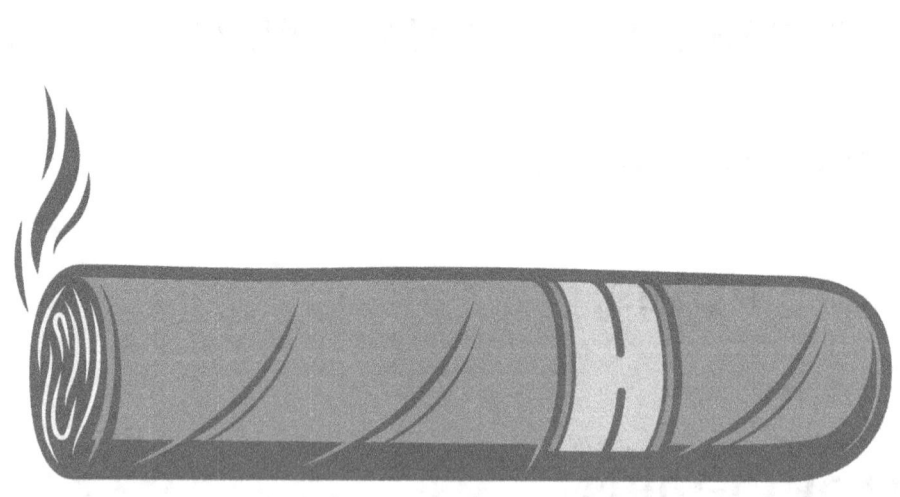

TODAY'S CIGAR:

SIZE/SHAPE:

COUNTRY OF ORIGIN:

APPEARANCE:

PRE-LIGHT:

LIGHTING:

FLAVORS:

FIRST THIRD-

SECOND THIRD-

FINAL THIRD-

STRENGTH: **MILD - MEDIUM - FULL**

BURN / DRAW:

NOTES:

GRADE (0-100):

TAPE YOUR CIGAR BAND HERE

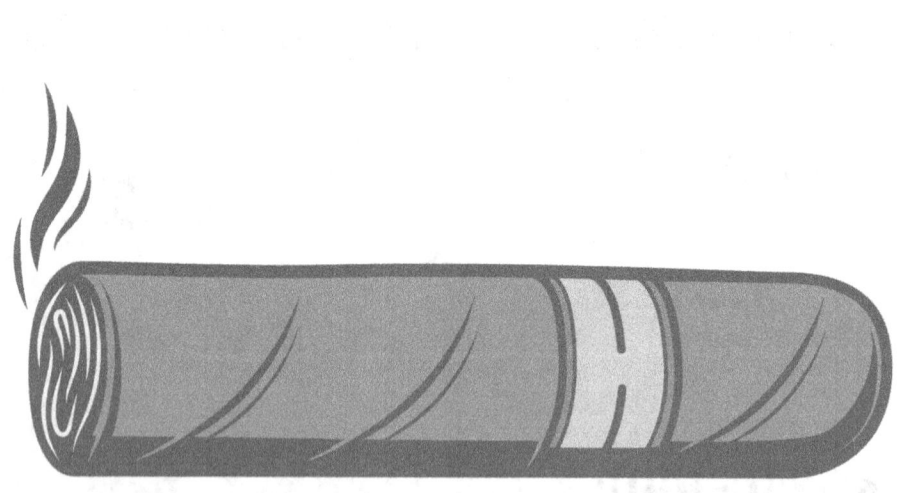

TODAY'S CIGAR:

SIZE/SHAPE:

COUNTRY OF ORIGIN:

APPEARANCE:

PRE-LIGHT:

LIGHTING:

FLAVORS:

FIRST THIRD-

SECOND THIRD-

FINAL THIRD-

STRENGTH: **MILD - MEDIUM - FULL**

BURN / DRAW:

NOTES:

GRADE (0-100):

TAPE YOUR CIGAR BAND HERE

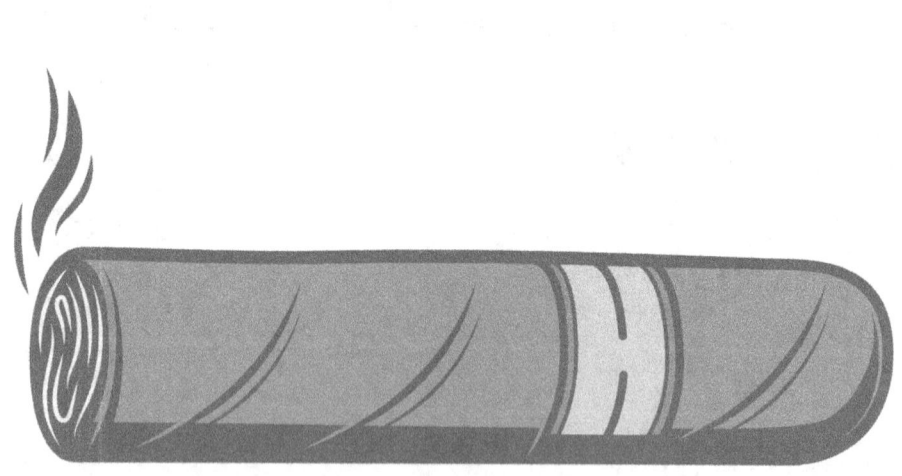

TODAY'S CIGAR:

SIZE/SHAPE:

COUNTRY OF ORIGIN:

APPEARANCE:

PRE-LIGHT:

LIGHTING:

FLAVORS:

FIRST THIRD-

SECOND THIRD-

FINAL THIRD-

STRENGTH: **MILD - MEDIUM - FULL**

BURN / DRAW:

NOTES:

GRADE (0-100):

TAPE YOUR CIGAR BAND HERE

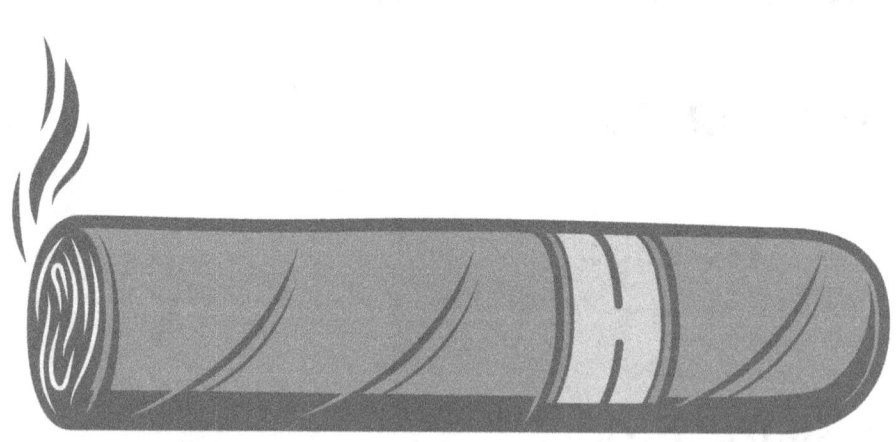

TODAY'S CIGAR:

SIZE/SHAPE:

COUNTRY OF ORIGIN:

APPEARANCE:

PRE-LIGHT:

LIGHTING:

FLAVORS:

FIRST THIRD-

SECOND THIRD-

FINAL THIRD-

STRENGTH: **MILD - MEDIUM - FULL**

BURN / DRAW:

NOTES:

GRADE (0-100):

TAPE YOUR CIGAR BAND HERE

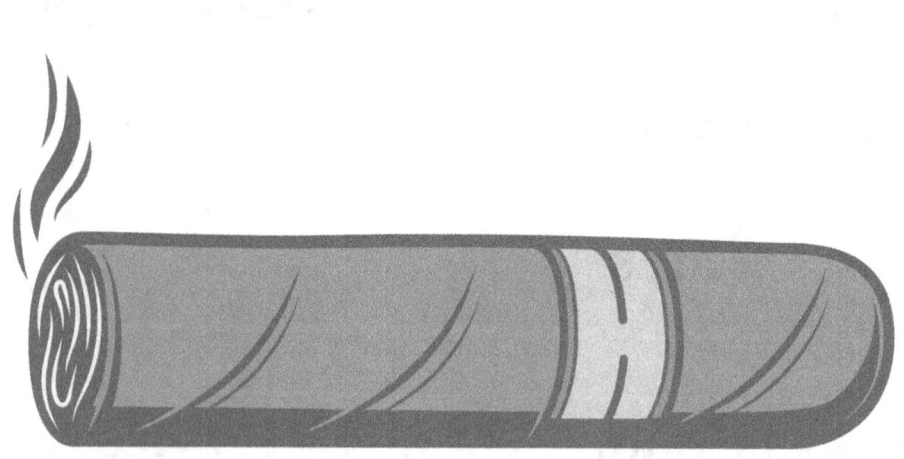

TODAY'S CIGAR:

SIZE/SHAPE:

COUNTRY OF ORIGIN:

APPEARANCE:

PRE-LIGHT:

LIGHTING:

FLAVORS:

FIRST THIRD-

SECOND THIRD-

FINAL THIRD-

STRENGTH: **MILD - MEDIUM - FULL**

BURN / DRAW:

NOTES:

GRADE (0-100):

TAPE YOUR CIGAR BAND HERE

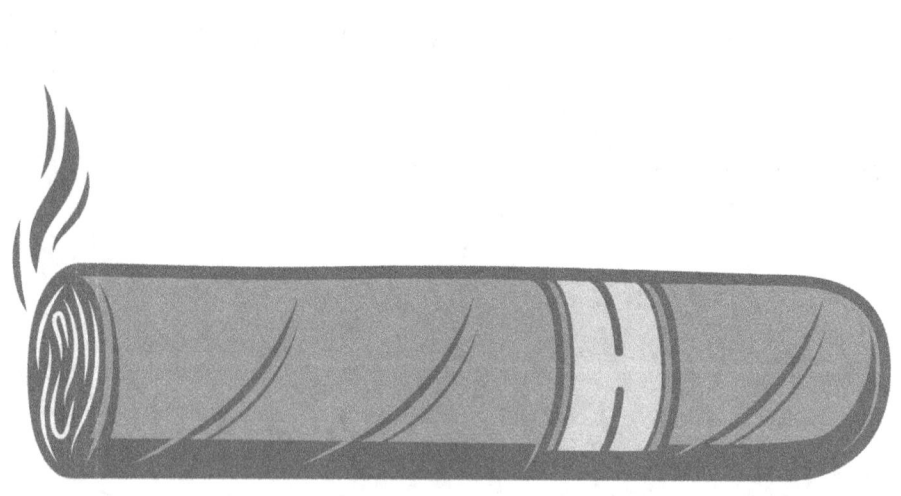

TODAY'S CIGAR:

SIZE/SHAPE:

COUNTRY OF ORIGIN:

APPEARANCE:

PRE-LIGHT:

LIGHTING:

FLAVORS:

FIRST THIRD-

SECOND THIRD-

FINAL THIRD-

STRENGTH: **MILD - MEDIUM - FULL**

BURN / DRAW:

NOTES:

GRADE (0-100):

TAPE YOUR CIGAR BAND HERE

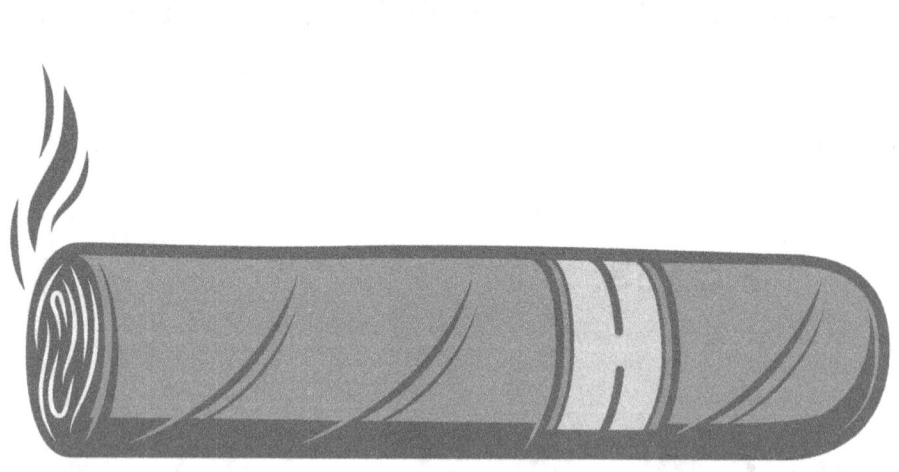

TODAY'S CIGAR:

SIZE/SHAPE:

COUNTRY OF ORIGIN:

APPEARANCE:

PRE-LIGHT:

LIGHTING:

FLAVORS:

FIRST THIRD-

SECOND THIRD-

FINAL THIRD-

STRENGTH: MILD - MEDIUM - FULL

BURN / DRAW:

NOTES:

GRADE (0-100):

TAPE YOUR CIGAR BAND HERE

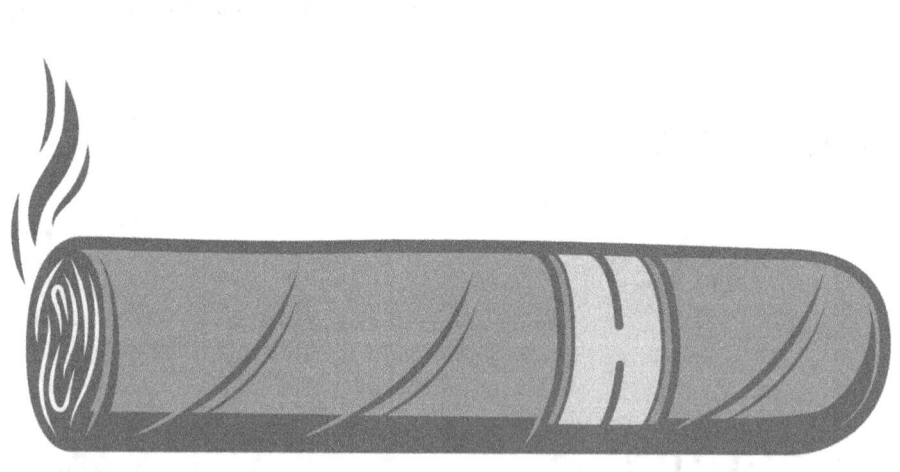

TODAY'S CIGAR:

SIZE/SHAPE:

COUNTRY OF ORIGIN:

APPEARANCE:

PRE-LIGHT:

LIGHTING:

FLAVORS:

FIRST THIRD-

SECOND THIRD-

FINAL THIRD-

STRENGTH: **MILD - MEDIUM - FULL**

BURN / DRAW:

NOTES:

GRADE (0-100):

TAPE YOUR CIGAR BAND HERE

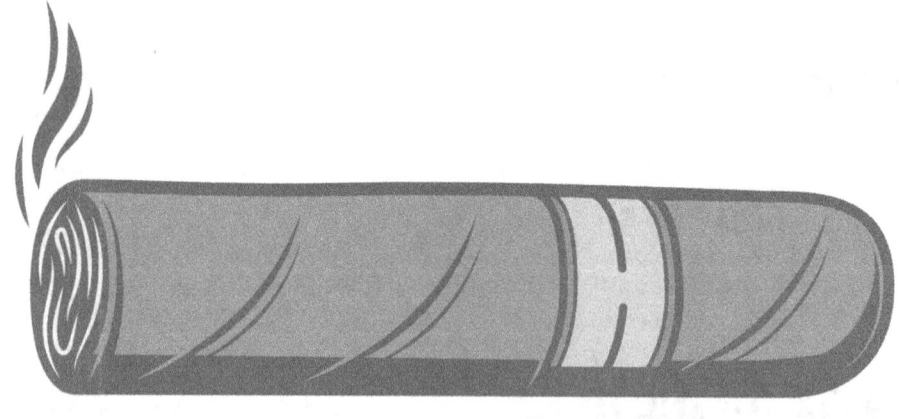

TODAY'S CIGAR:

SIZE/SHAPE:

COUNTRY OF ORIGIN:

APPEARANCE:

PRE-LIGHT:

LIGHTING:

FLAVORS:

FIRST THIRD-

SECOND THIRD-

FINAL THIRD-

STRENGTH: **MILD - MEDIUM - FULL**

BURN / DRAW:

NOTES:

GRADE (0-100):

TAPE YOUR CIGAR BAND HERE

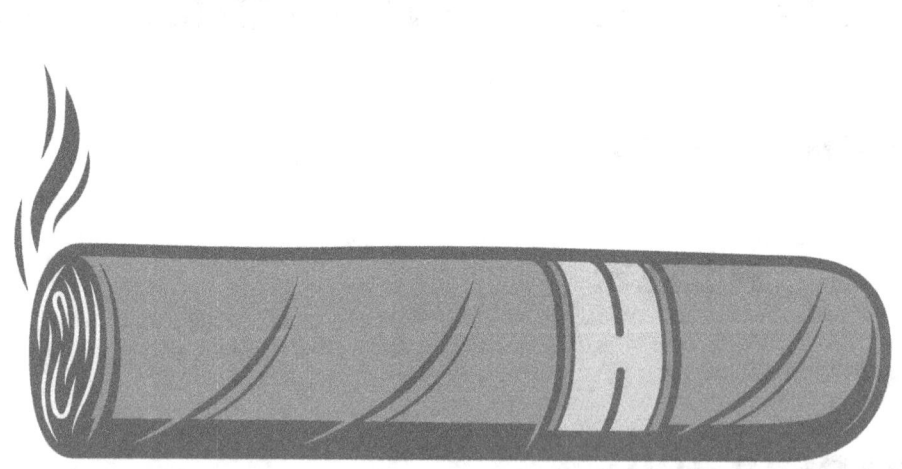

TODAY'S CIGAR:

SIZE/SHAPE:

COUNTRY OF ORIGIN:

APPEARANCE:

PRE-LIGHT:

LIGHTING:

FLAVORS:

FIRST THIRD-

SECOND THIRD-

FINAL THIRD-

STRENGTH: **MILD - MEDIUM - FULL**

BURN / DRAW:

NOTES:

GRADE (0-100):

TAPE YOUR CIGAR BAND HERE

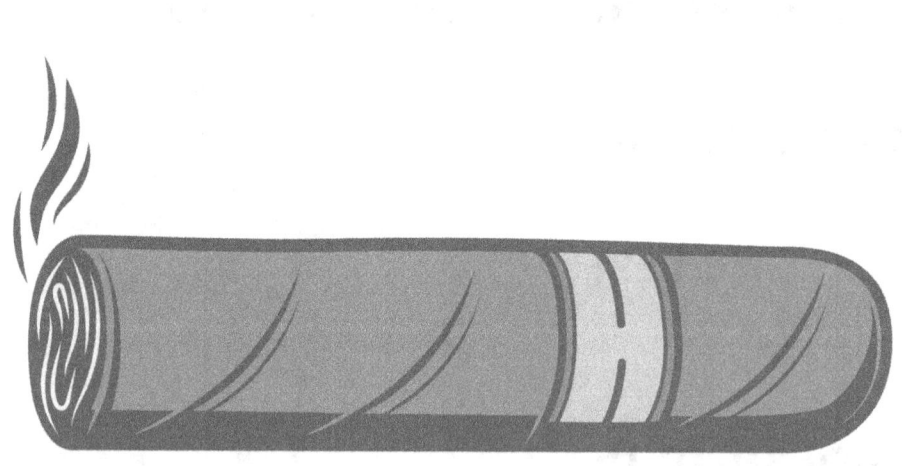

TODAY'S CIGAR:

SIZE/SHAPE:

COUNTRY OF ORIGIN:

APPEARANCE:

PRE-LIGHT:

LIGHTING:

FLAVORS:

FIRST THIRD-

SECOND THIRD-

FINAL THIRD-

STRENGTH: **MILD - MEDIUM - FULL**

BURN / DRAW:

NOTES:

GRADE (0-100):

TAPE YOUR CIGAR BAND HERE

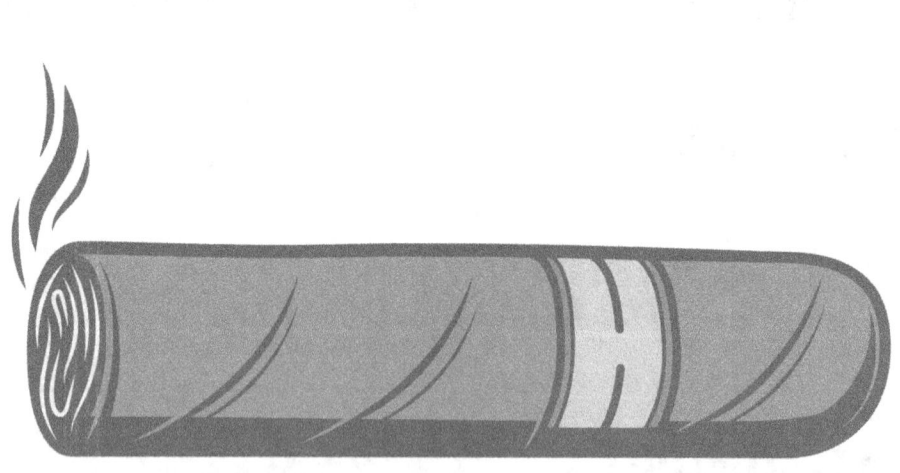

TODAY'S CIGAR:

SIZE/SHAPE:

COUNTRY OF ORIGIN:

APPEARANCE:

PRE-LIGHT:

LIGHTING:

FLAVORS:

FIRST THIRD-

SECOND THIRD-

FINAL THIRD-

STRENGTH: MILD - MEDIUM - FULL

BURN / DRAW:

NOTES:

GRADE (0-100):

TAPE YOUR CIGAR BAND HERE

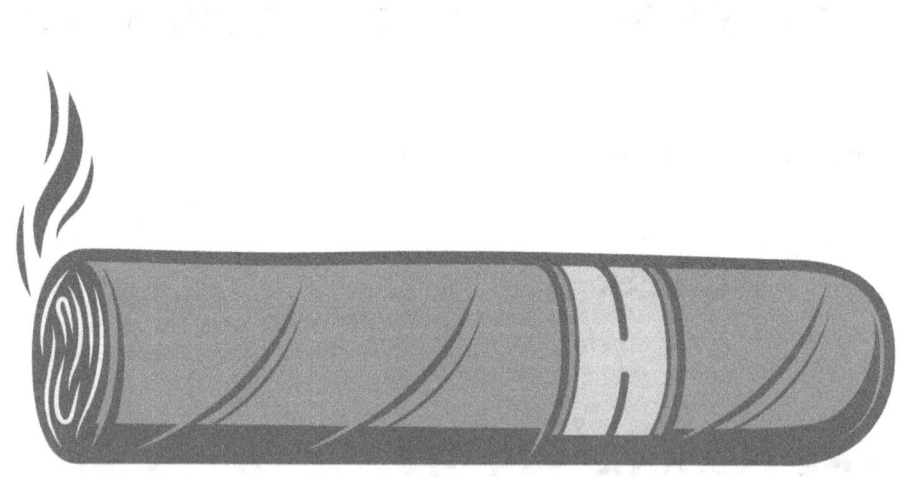

TODAY'S CIGAR:

SIZE/SHAPE:

COUNTRY OF ORIGIN:

APPEARANCE:

PRE-LIGHT:

LIGHTING:

FLAVORS:

FIRST THIRD-

SECOND THIRD-

FINAL THIRD-

STRENGTH: **MILD - MEDIUM - FULL**

BURN / DRAW:

NOTES:

GRADE (0-100):

TAPE YOUR CIGAR BAND HERE

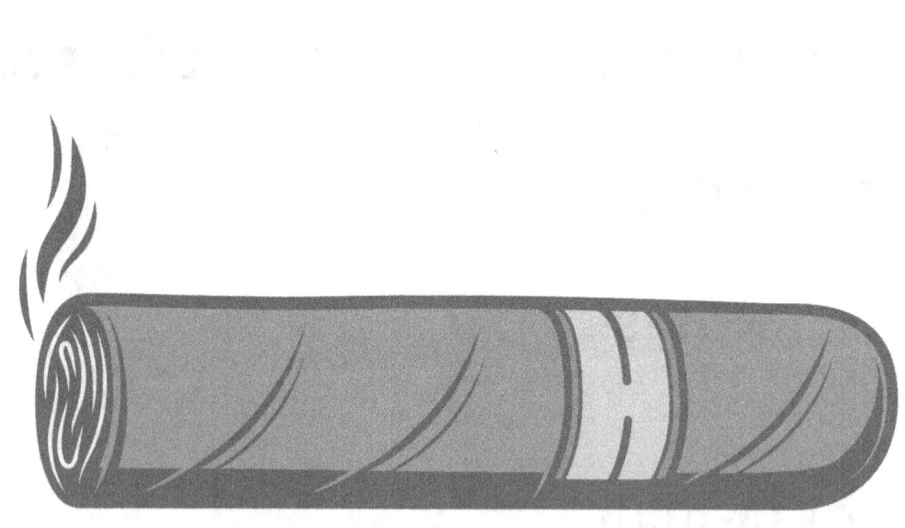

TODAY'S CIGAR:

SIZE/SHAPE:

COUNTRY OF ORIGIN:

APPEARANCE:

PRE-LIGHT:

LIGHTING:

FLAVORS:

FIRST THIRD-

SECOND THIRD-

FINAL THIRD-

STRENGTH: **MILD - MEDIUM - FULL**

BURN / DRAW:

NOTES:

GRADE (0-100):

TAPE YOUR CIGAR BAND HERE

TODAY'S CIGAR:

SIZE/SHAPE:

COUNTRY OF ORIGIN:

APPEARANCE:

PRE-LIGHT:

LIGHTING:

FLAVORS:

FIRST THIRD-

SECOND THIRD-

FINAL THIRD-

STRENGTH: MILD - MEDIUM - FULL

BURN / DRAW:

NOTES:

GRADE (0-100):

TAPE YOUR CIGAR BAND HERE

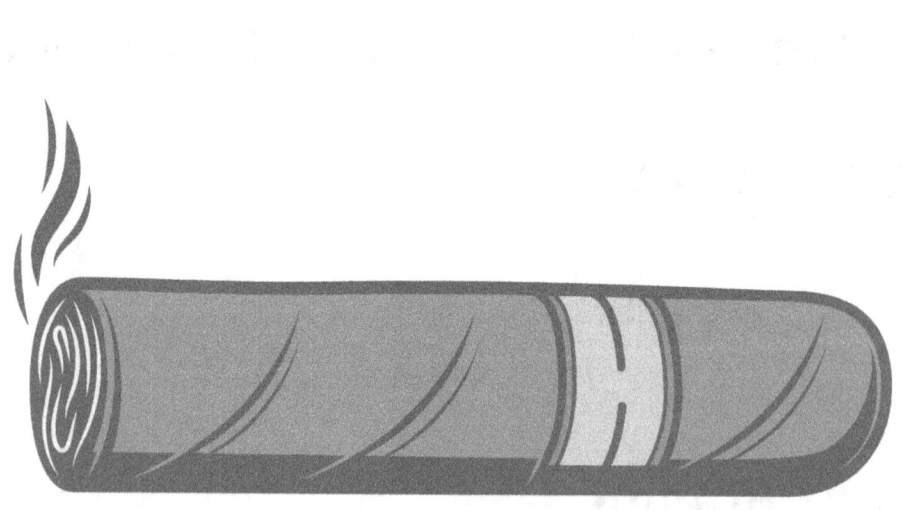

TODAY'S CIGAR:

SIZE/SHAPE:

COUNTRY OF ORIGIN:

APPEARANCE:

PRE-LIGHT:

LIGHTING:

FLAVORS:

FIRST THIRD-

SECOND THIRD-

FINAL THIRD-

STRENGTH: MILD - MEDIUM - FULL

BURN / DRAW:

NOTES:

GRADE (0-100):

TAPE YOUR CIGAR BAND HERE

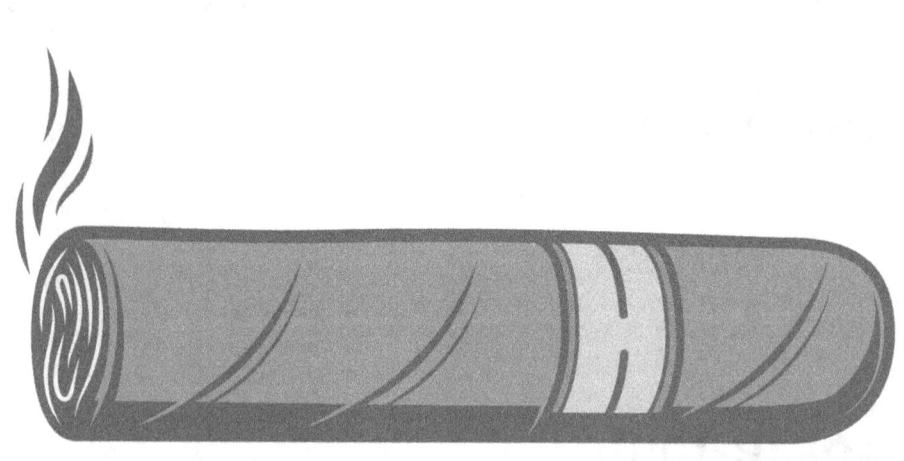

TODAY'S CIGAR:

SIZE/SHAPE:

COUNTRY OF ORIGIN:

APPEARANCE:

PRE-LIGHT:

LIGHTING:

FLAVORS:

FIRST THIRD-

SECOND THIRD-

FINAL THIRD-

STRENGTH: **MILD - MEDIUM - FULL**

BURN / DRAW:

NOTES:

GRADE (0-100):

TAPE YOUR CIGAR BAND HERE

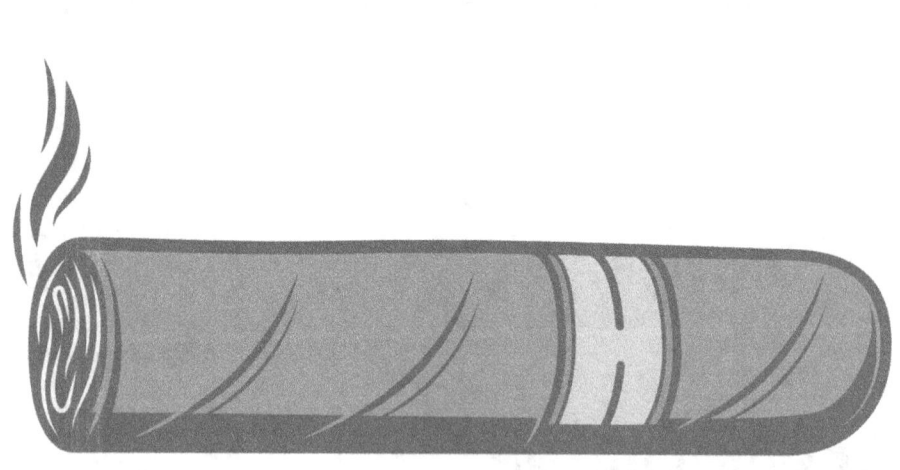

TODAY'S CIGAR:

SIZE/SHAPE:

COUNTRY OF ORIGIN:

APPEARANCE:

PRE-LIGHT:

LIGHTING:

FLAVORS:

FIRST THIRD-

SECOND THIRD-

FINAL THIRD-

STRENGTH: **MILD - MEDIUM - FULL**

BURN / DRAW:

NOTES:

GRADE (0-100):

TAPE YOUR CIGAR BAND HERE

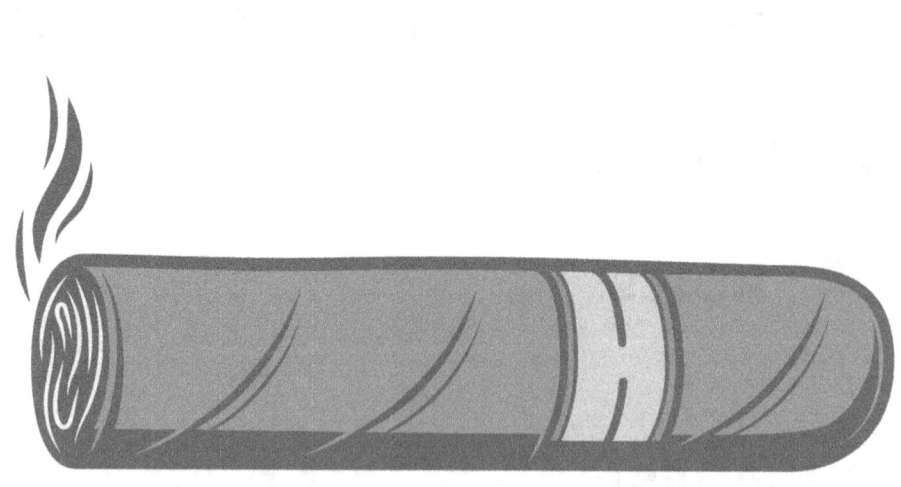

TODAY'S CIGAR:

SIZE/SHAPE:

COUNTRY OF ORIGIN:

APPEARANCE:

PRE-LIGHT:

LIGHTING:

FLAVORS:

FIRST THIRD-

SECOND THIRD-

FINAL THIRD-

STRENGTH: **MILD - MEDIUM - FULL**

BURN / DRAW:

NOTES:

GRADE (0-100):

TAPE YOUR CIGAR BAND HERE

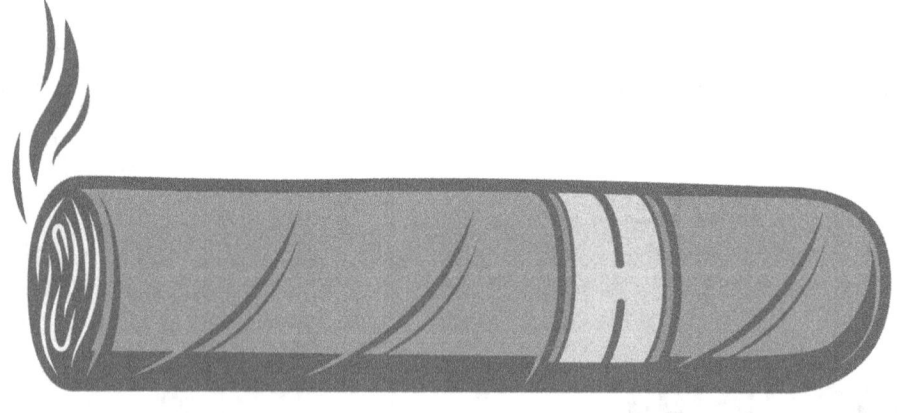

TODAY'S CIGAR:

SIZE/SHAPE:

COUNTRY OF ORIGIN:

APPEARANCE:

PRE-LIGHT:

LIGHTING:

FLAVORS:

FIRST THIRD-

SECOND THIRD-

FINAL THIRD-

STRENGTH: **MILD - MEDIUM - FULL**

BURN / DRAW:

NOTES:

GRADE (0-100):

TAPE YOUR CIGAR BAND HERE

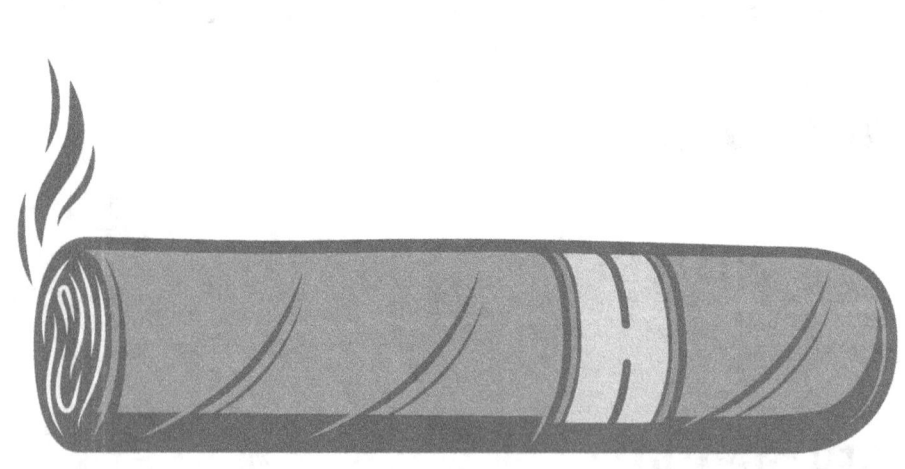

TODAY'S CIGAR:

SIZE/SHAPE:

COUNTRY OF ORIGIN:

APPEARANCE:

PRE-LIGHT:

LIGHTING:

FLAVORS:

FIRST THIRD-

SECOND THIRD-

FINAL THIRD-

STRENGTH: **MILD - MEDIUM - FULL**

BURN / DRAW:

NOTES:

GRADE (0-100):

TAPE YOUR CIGAR BAND HERE

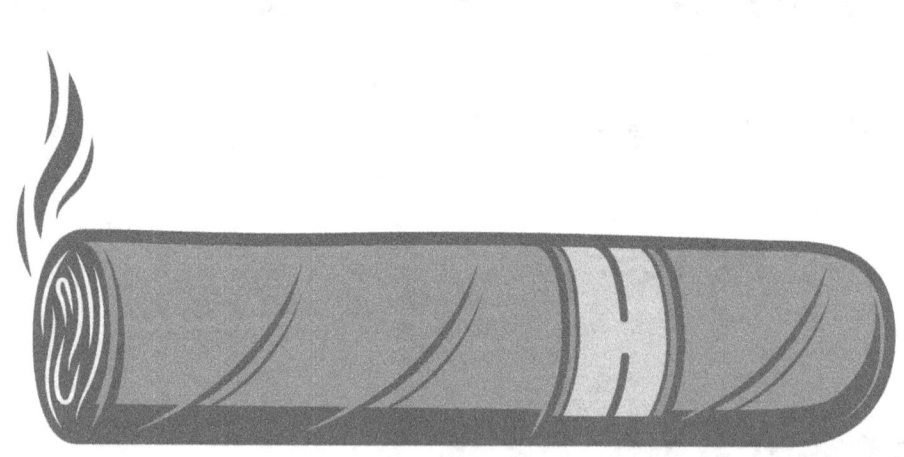

TODAY'S CIGAR:

SIZE/SHAPE:

COUNTRY OF ORIGIN:

APPEARANCE:

PRE-LIGHT:

LIGHTING:

FLAVORS:
FIRST THIRD-
SECOND THIRD-
FINAL THIRD-

STRENGTH: **MILD - MEDIUM - FULL**

BURN / DRAW:

NOTES:

GRADE (0-100):

TAPE YOUR CIGAR BAND HERE

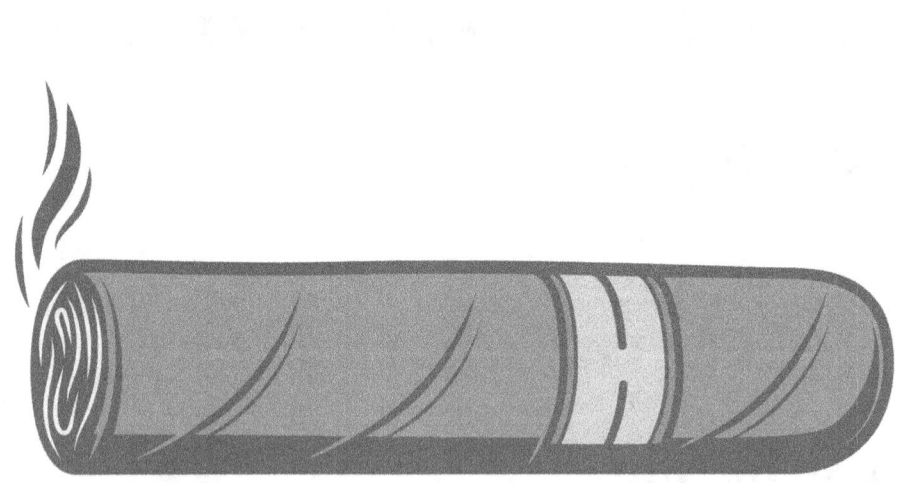

TODAY'S CIGAR:

SIZE/SHAPE:

COUNTRY OF ORIGIN:

APPEARANCE:

PRE-LIGHT:

LIGHTING:

FLAVORS:

FIRST THIRD-

SECOND THIRD-

FINAL THIRD-

STRENGTH: **MILD - MEDIUM - FULL**

BURN / DRAW:

NOTES:

GRADE (0-100):

TAPE YOUR CIGAR BAND HERE

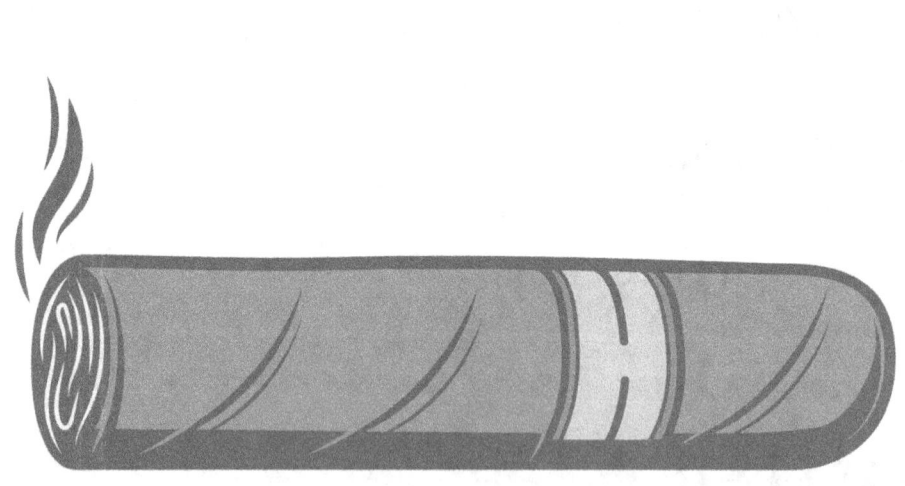

TODAY'S CIGAR:

SIZE/SHAPE:

COUNTRY OF ORIGIN:

APPEARANCE:

PRE-LIGHT:

LIGHTING:

FLAVORS:

FIRST THIRD-

SECOND THIRD-

FINAL THIRD-

STRENGTH: **MILD - MEDIUM - FULL**

BURN / DRAW:

NOTES:

GRADE (0-100):

TAPE YOUR CIGAR BAND HERE

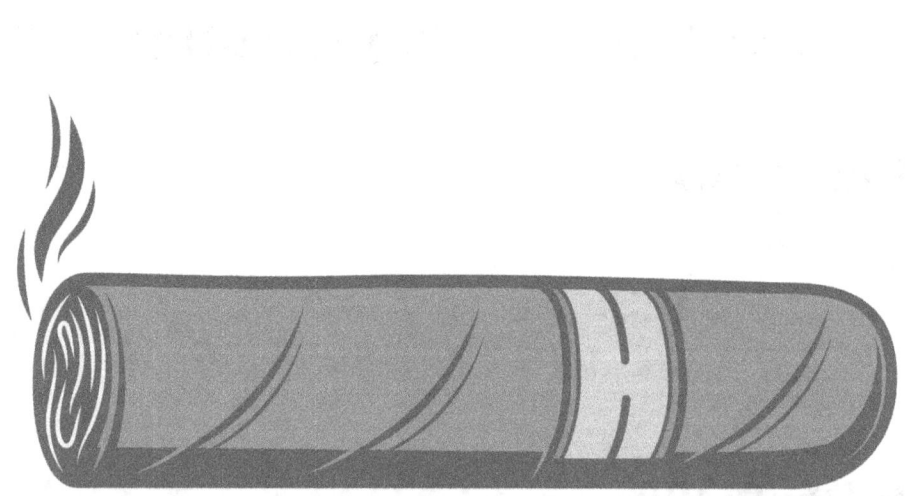

TODAY'S CIGAR:

SIZE/SHAPE:

COUNTRY OF ORIGIN:

APPEARANCE:

PRE-LIGHT:

LIGHTING:

FLAVORS:

FIRST THIRD-

SECOND THIRD-

FINAL THIRD-

STRENGTH: MILD - MEDIUM - FULL

BURN / DRAW:

NOTES:

GRADE (0-100):

TAPE YOUR CIGAR BAND HERE

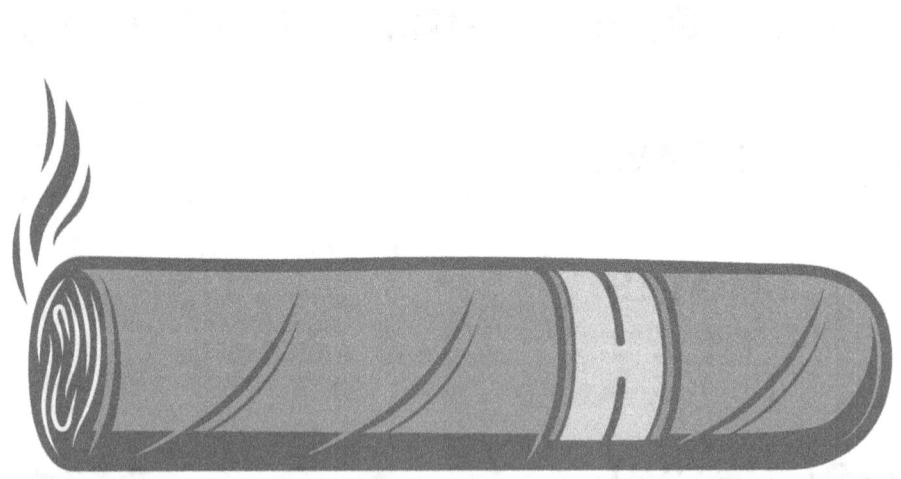

TODAY'S CIGAR:

SIZE/SHAPE:
COUNTRY OF ORIGIN:

APPEARANCE:
PRE-LIGHT:
LIGHTING:

FLAVORS:
FIRST THIRD-
SECOND THIRD-
FINAL THIRD-

STRENGTH: MILD - MEDIUM - FULL

BURN / DRAW:

NOTES:

GRADE (0-100):

TAPE YOUR CIGAR BAND HERE

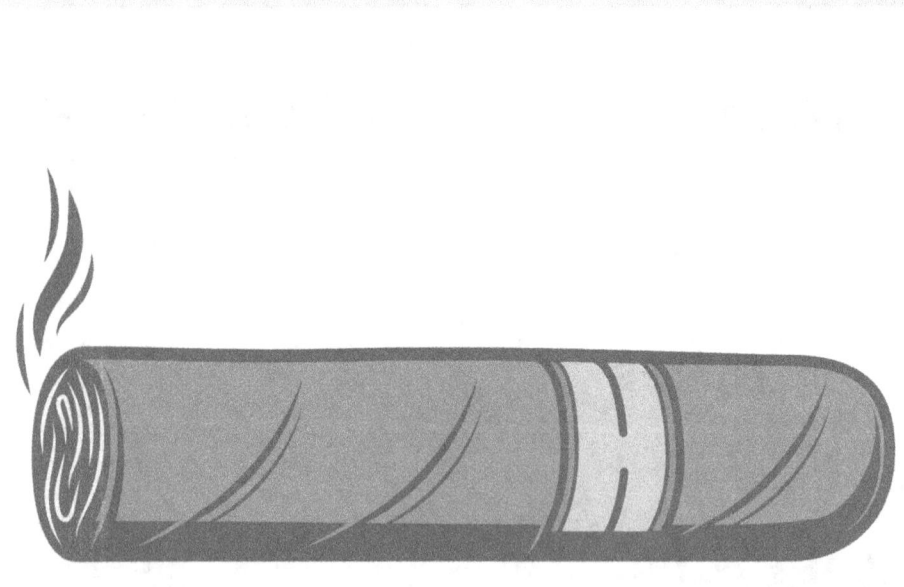

TODAY'S CIGAR:

SIZE/SHAPE:

COUNTRY OF ORIGIN:

APPEARANCE:

PRE-LIGHT:

LIGHTING:

FLAVORS:
FIRST THIRD-
SECOND THIRD-
FINAL THIRD-

STRENGTH: **MILD - MEDIUM - FULL**

BURN / DRAW:

NOTES:

GRADE (0-100):

TAPE YOUR CIGAR BAND HERE

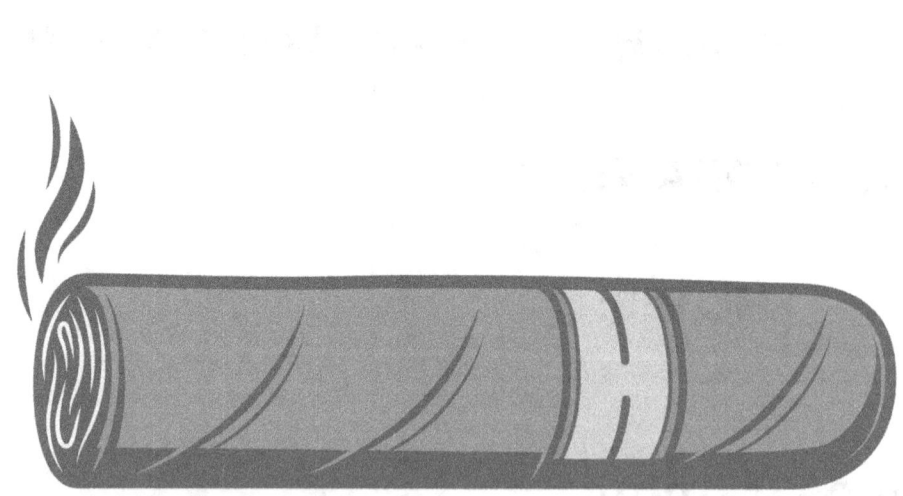

TODAY'S CIGAR:

SIZE/SHAPE:

COUNTRY OF ORIGIN:

APPEARANCE:

PRE-LIGHT:

LIGHTING:

FLAVORS:

FIRST THIRD-

SECOND THIRD-

FINAL THIRD-

STRENGTH: **MILD - MEDIUM - FULL**

BURN / DRAW:

NOTES:

GRADE (0-100):

Cigar Smoker FAQ

What are the mechanics of smoking a cigar? Tell me how to clip it. Do I remove the band? How do I light it? How do I deal with the ash? What do I do with the cigar when I'm finished? Help!

So, here are the mechanics of smoking a cigar:

- Clipping the cigar: Before lighting your cigar, you'll need to clip off the cap at the end of the cigar. You can use a cigar cutter to make a clean, straight cut. Try to avoid cutting too much of the cap, or the cigar may unravel.
- Removing the band: Some people prefer to remove the band before smoking the cigar, while others

leave it on. If you choose to remove the band, do so carefully to avoid damaging the wrapper.

- Lighting the cigar: Use a butane lighter or a wooden match to light the foot of the cigar. Hold the flame just under the foot and rotate the cigar until it's evenly lit. Don't inhale the smoke; just draw it into your mouth.

- Dealing with the ash: As you smoke the cigar, ash will accumulate on the end. Roll the ash off gently into an ashtray rather than flicking it off.

- Smoking the cigar: Take your time and enjoy the flavors of the cigar. Don't inhale the smoke, as this can cause irritation or even make you sick.

- Disposing of the cigar: When you're done smoking, dispose of the cigar butt in an ashtray or other appropriate receptacle. Don't snub it out like a cigarette; that creates a foul smell. And don't toss it on the ground or in the trash, as it can still be hot and could start a fire.

I want to bring cigars to a friend's barbecue. What do I do?

When selecting cigars to bring to a party with both experienced and less experienced cigar smokers, it's important to find a balance between quality and accessibility. Here are a few tips to help you make a good selection:

- Consider the occasion: Since this is a barbecue, you may want to consider bringing cigars that pair well with the food and drinks that will be served. For example, if there will be a lot of grilled meats, a medium-bodied cigar with a woody or spicy profile may be a good option.

- Look for versatile options: Choose cigars that are well-rounded and appeal to a broad range of tastes. A medium-bodied cigar with a smooth and creamy profile, for example, can be a good option for both experienced and less experienced smokers.

- Pay attention to size: Consider bringing cigars in a range of sizes so that your guests can choose a cigar that suits their preference. For example, you might bring a mix of larger and smaller cigars, or a few different sizes of the same blend.

- Bring a variety: Consider bringing a mix of different blends, so that your guests can try a few different flavors and find one that they enjoy.

Some specific cigar recommendations that might be a good fit for your barbecue include the Arturo Fuente Hemingway, which has a medium body and a smooth, creamy profile, or the Padron 1964 Anniversary Series, which is a little stronger but still accessible to less experienced smokers. Both of these options are well-regarded by experienced cigar smokers, but also offer a balanced flavor profile that is likely to appeal to a wider audience.

Ultimately, the best way to choose cigars to bring to a barbecue is to think about the occasion and the preferences of your guests. With a little planning and consideration, you can choose cigars that will be a hit with everyone at the party.

I'm going to a cigar lounge for the first time; what are the dos and don'ts?

Congratulations on being invited to a cigar lounge! It can be an exciting and enjoyable experience, but it's important to be aware of the etiquette and rules of the lounge in order to make the most of your visit. Here are some general tips on cigar lounge etiquette:

- Follow the dress code: Many cigar lounges have a dress code, which can range from business casual to more formal attire. Be sure to check the dress code ahead of time and dress accordingly.
- Respect other patrons: Cigar lounges are a place to relax and enjoy a cigar in peace. Be mindful of other patrons and keep your voice down.
- Buy cigars from the lounge. Even if you brought your own cigars to smoke, it's customary to purchase cigars from the establishment. In fact, some lounges will only allow cigars bought on-site.
- Use the ashtrays: Cigar smoke and ash can be messy, so be sure to use the ashtrays provided in the

lounge. Don't ash on the floor or on any other surface.

Remember that every cigar lounge may have slightly different rules and expectations, so be sure to familiarize yourself with the specific etiquette of the lounge you're visiting. And most importantly, relax, enjoy your cigar, and be respectful of others.

I'm new to cigars, and there are so many options. Just tell me what cigars to try!

As a new cigar smoker, you may want to start with a milder cigar to ease into the experience. Here are a few suggestions:

- Connecticut Shade: Connecticut Shade cigars are known for their mild to medium strength and smooth, creamy flavor. They're a good option for those who are new to cigars.
- Dominican Republic: Cigars from the Dominican Republic tend to be milder in strength and offer a smooth smoking experience. Many new cigar smokers start with a Dominican cigar.
- Macanudo: Macanudo cigars are a classic choice for new smokers. They are known for their mildness, smoothness, and consistent flavor profile.
- Arturo Fuente: Arturo Fuente cigars are also a popular choice for new smokers. They offer a range

of strengths and flavors, but many of their cigars are
on the milder side.

- Romeo y Julieta: Romeo y Julieta cigars are another
classic option for new smokers. They offer mild to
medium strength and a smooth smoking
experience.

Of course, everyone's tastes are different, so don't be afraid
to try a few different cigars to find the one that suits you best.
And remember, taking notes on each cigar you try can help you
remember what you liked and didn't like about each one, so you
can refine your preferences over time.

CONCLUSION

I hope you've enjoyed this book, and you're already filling it up with notes on your favorite sticks. And, I hope you're enjoying cigars with friends, because that's what it's really all about.

If you enjoyed this book, would you take a moment to leave a review? It's wildly helpful getting this book out to new audiences. And please post images of your fill-out pages; we'd all love to see your reviews.

Happy Smoking, amigos.

Greg

www.ingramcontent.com/pod-product-compliance
Lightning Source LLC
Chambersburg PA
CBHW071012120626
46546CB00003B/1051